21 DAY

Daniel Fast

Recipe Cookbook

127 EASY PLANT BASED RECIPES
WITH 4 WEEK MEAL PLAN

MARIA TARNEV-WYDRO, HD

Published by DanielFast.org

Copyright © 2021 by Maria Tarnev-Wydro, HD.

Printed in USA

www.DanielFast.org

"You will seek me and find me when you seek me with all your heart." Jeremiah 29:13

Daniel Fast.org

TABLE OF CONTENTS

Other Books by Maria

Emotional Rescue
Conversation with My Lord
My Path to Holiness

15 Healthiest Green Superfoods
Daniel Fast Workbook
Daniel Fast Workbook 2

All books available at

Daniel Fast.org

or

amazon.com

Meet the Author

Maria Tarnev-Wydro, HD, is a mother of 3 children, wife, and the founder of DanielFast.org. She has a passionate evangelic gift to help others understand true salvation through Jesus Christ. Maria writes books about faith, nutrition, holistic beauty, healthy cooking, and healing.

"My mission is to inspire and empower each of you to take steps to restore your health, transform your life, renew your mind, and unlock your God-given potential. "

God Bless,

Maria

WELCOME TO THE DANIEL FAST RECIPE COOKBOOK

This is a companion book that is best used in conjunction with the *21 Day Daniel Fast Workbook: Daily Prayer Journal* by Maria Tarnev-Wydro, HD. This book provides delicious and easy-to-prepare meals, dips, salads and more that you can eat while on the Daniel Fast. It also includes 4 suggested meal plans in the Appendix for you to follow if you wish. You can use the meal plans as a starting point if you are new to the Daniel Fast. As you become more comfortable with the fast, you can create your own delightful meals.

Each recipe has complete nutritional information in case you need this information for your specific health status. All recipes are made with wholesome, fresh foods that are bursting with nutrients your body will love. We have tried to incorporate recipes from many different cuisines from around the world so you can have fun and share new tastes with your friends. Take photos of your inspired creations and show them to your friends to share the enjoyment. The important thing to remember is that it is not a weight loss diet, it is a time of prayer and fasting to draw nearer to God. Any weight loss or increase in energy is just a bonus.

WHO IS DANIEL?

The story about Daniel surviving in the lion's den is not the only amazing story about Daniel in the Bible. He is also known for his commitment to fasting and prayer while under great persecution. Daniel was a member of the royal elite in Israel (Judah) in the 6th century BC when Judah was conquered by the Assyrians and King Nebuchadnezzar. He was taken from his home in Judah and sent to be trained in the ways of the Babylonians and serve in the court of King Nebuchadnezzar because he was well educated, bright and noble. He eventually ended up being appointed as the ruler over the entire province of Babylon and the king placed him in charge of all its wise men.

Daniel was a prophet, not only for his time, but also for the end times and served under 4 different kings. During his service to the kings, he never compromised his faith in God and always prayed and fasted during difficult situations. . The first time Daniel fasted and prayed was in Daniel, Chapter 1:3-15, and It was for ten days. The second time Daniel fasted and prayed was for 21 days to enable Daniel to hear God more clearly—to bring his body under the control of the spirit rather than the other way around. Both times, however, Daniel's fasting was for the glory of God.

WHAT IS PRAYER AND FASTING?

Prayer and fasting can be simply described as a dedicated time with God where you enter into single-minded devotion. Your mind becomes zoned in on Him and His will for your life. Prayer and fasting focus on:

1. Gratitude, which is intentional prayer.
2. Praise, which ushers you into the presence of God.
3. Worship, which is our ultimate goal. In worship, we surrender to God.
4. Seeking God's will.
5. Spiritual healing and transformation from "the old man" to "the new man.

Through prayer and fasting you will let go of your issues and focus on God. He is calling you to fast for a specific reason or purpose. Trust Him. In this place, you position yourself to receive a breakthrough and the release of miracles. During your fast, you will sense the presence of the Lord and the Holy Spirit refreshing your soul and spirit. We are created for communion with God. Run to him when you're feeling down and discouraged. Cry out to him when you feel overwhelmed, hurt and wounded. God loves you! When you love him back, you experience full freedom.

DESCRIPTION OF THE DANIEL FAST

The "Daniel Fast" is a partial fast, similar to the whole-food, plant-based diet practiced by Adam and Eve in the Garden of Eden. Today, some would refer to it as a vegan diet, but the Daniel Fast has more restrictions. For example: not only are meat, fish and dairy forbidden, but also sugar, sweeteners, yeast, coffee, alcohol, processed foods are not allowed as well.

"I ate no choice food; no meat or wine

touched my lips."

- Daniel 10:3a.

The good news is that you can eat all the fresh fruits, vegetables, legumes, nuts, seeds, whole grains and drink all the water you want.

What To Eat During Daniel Fast
21 Days Daniel Fast Food List

FOODS TO EAT — yes!

ALL FRUITS
(fresh, frozen, dried, juiced, or canned)
Apples, Apricots, Avocados, Bananas, Blackberries, Blueberries, Cantaloupe, Cherries, Coconuts, Cranberries, Dates, Figs, Grapefruit, Grapes, Guava, Honeydew melons, Kiwi, Lemons, Limes, Mangoes, Melons, Nectarines, Oranges, Papayas, Peaches, Pears, Pineapples, Plums, Prunes, Raisins, Raspberries, Strawberries, Tangerines, Watermelon.

ALL WHOLE GRAINS
(preferably organic)
Amaranth, Barley, Brown rice, Millet, Quinoa, Oats (groats soaked), Whole Wheat.

ALL LEGUMES
(preferably organic, raw, unsalted and soaked/sprouted) †
Black beans, Black eyed peas, Cannellini beans, Garbanzo beans (chickpeas), Great northern beans, Kidney beans, Lentils, Mung beans, Pinto beans, and Split peas.

BEVERAGES
Water, Homemade Vegetable juice, Green Smoothies, Homemade Nuts Milks.

ALL VEGETABLES
(fresh, frozen, dried, juiced, or canned)
Artichokes, Asparagus, Beets, Broccoli, Brussel sprouts, Cabbage, Carrots, Cauliflower, Celery, Collard greens, Corn, Cucumbers, Eggplant, Green beans, Kale, Leeks, Lettuce, Mushrooms, Mustard greens, Okra, Onions, Parsley, Peppers, Potatoes, Radishes, Rutabagas, Scallions, Spinach, Sprouts, Squash, Sweet potatoes, Tomatoes, Turnips, Yams, Zucchini.

ALL QUALITY OILS
Avocado, Coconut, Grapeseed, Olive, Peanut, Sesame, and Walnut.

SPICES AND CONDIMENTS
Herbs, Spices, Salt, Pepper, Seasonings, Braggís Liquid Aminos.

ALL NUTS & SEEDS
(preferably organic, raw, unsalted and soaked/sprouted)
All nuts (raw, unsalted), Almonds, Cashews, Chia seed, Flaxseed, Macadamia nuts, Peanuts, Pecans, Pine nuts, Walnuts, Pumpkin seeds, Sesame seeds, and Sunflower seeds; Unsweetened almond milk. Nut butters are also included.

FOODS TO AVOID — no!

All Meat & Animal Products
Bacon, Beef, Buffalo, Eggs, Fish, Lamb, Poultry, Pork.

All Dairy Products
Butter, Cheese, Cream, Milk, Yogurt.

All Sweeteners
Agave Nectar, Artificial Sweeteners, Brown Rice Syrup, Cane Juice, Honey, Molasses, Raw Sugar, Syrups, Stevia, Sugar.

All Leavened Bread & Yeast
Baked Goods & Bread.

All Refined & Processed Food Products
Artificial Flavorings, Chemicals, Food Additives, Preservatives, White Flour, White Rice.

All Deep-Fried Foods†
Corn Chips, French Fries, Potato Chips. All Solid Fats Lard, Margarine, and Shortening.

Beverages
Alcohol, Carbonated Drinks, Coffee, Energy Drinks, Teas.

TIPS AND SUGGESTIONS

1. Please read the recipe before you start to make sure you have all the proper ingredients.

2. If you have allergies or sensitivities to any ingredient in a recipe, omit it or use a suitable substitute.

3. Don't assume all vegan foods are part of the Daniel Fast. Check labels and ingredients. Learn to read the food labels and make sure you know what you are eating.

4. Feel free to be creative and adjust any recipe to your specific tastes. Start with dishes that you are familiar with and expand your tastes.

5. Make sure you drink plenty of fresh, clean water every day to flush away toxins.

6. When cooking your foods, steaming, baking, grilling, roasting and water sauté are the best cooking methods during Daniel Fast Avoid frying or stir-frying.

7. Use fresh fruits and vegetables as often as possible. Organic is the best choice and buy from farmers markets. Thoroughly wash all fruits and veggies before using.

8. You can cut up the ingredients for several smoothies at once and store them in plastic ziplock bags in the freezer for later use.

9. When making smoothies, it is best to have a blend of fruits and vegetables to balance sweetness. Smoothies made only with fruits tend to be too sweet and can spike your insulin level.

10. Always choose whole grains

11. When using beans, lentils and nuts, it is best to soak them overnight, drain them and discard the water before using.

12. You can boil quinoa, beans, lentils and chickpeas and store them for several days in airtight containers in your refrigerator for immediate use in salads, soups, stews, Paradise Garden Bowls, etc.

13. In order to thicken any stews or soups, you can use flaxseed meal, ground oatmeal, mashed potato, veggie puree or ground chia seeds.

14. If recipes call for nut milk, you can make your own by blending 1 -part presoaked nuts with 2- parts water and adding a pinch of salt.

15. You can roast nuts, seeds, chickpeas with different spice mixes and take with them anywhere you go as a quick, tasty snack.

16. You can avoid frying by making your own roasted or raw garlic, ginger and/or onion paste. Grind it, mix with a little oil into a paste consistency and store in air tight container in the refrigerator. Add to recipe as needed instead of sautéing fresh.

17. You can make your own veggie noodles using a zucchini spiralizer

18. To prevent your cutting board from slipping place a wet paper towel underneath.

19. Use a teaspoon to easily peel ginger.

20. To prevent cut vegetables from oxidizing and turning brown by storing them in cold water.

21. For baked burgers you want to do the following for less crumbly burgers. First, mash the ingredients well and use finely chopped veggies. Larger veggies or beans make the patties crumbly. Next, keep the dough moist. You may add 1 flax egg. (1 tbsp. flaxmeal in 3 tbsp. water) or more to substitute for the binding property of egg.

22. Veggie/bean burgers should be frozen before baking. Shape the patties and freeze on a baking sheet. When frozen, you can place them in a ziplock or other container, separated by parchment. Remove from freezer and bake or grill.

23. To prepere jackfruit, drain your jackfruit, place it in a cheese cloth, squeeze out the brine. Use your hands to break it into shreds that resemble pulled pork or shredded chicken.

24. Tomato paste, stock, and sauces can be frozen into ice cubes and easily defrosted for recipes.

25. Black pepper should be aadded at the end. Black pepper burns at 325f.

26. Always cook your mushrooms. Chopping mushrooms helps further break down the chitin and assists in unlocking nutritional content.

27. Switch To Kosher, Himalayan or Sea Salt.

Enjoy and Bon Appétit!

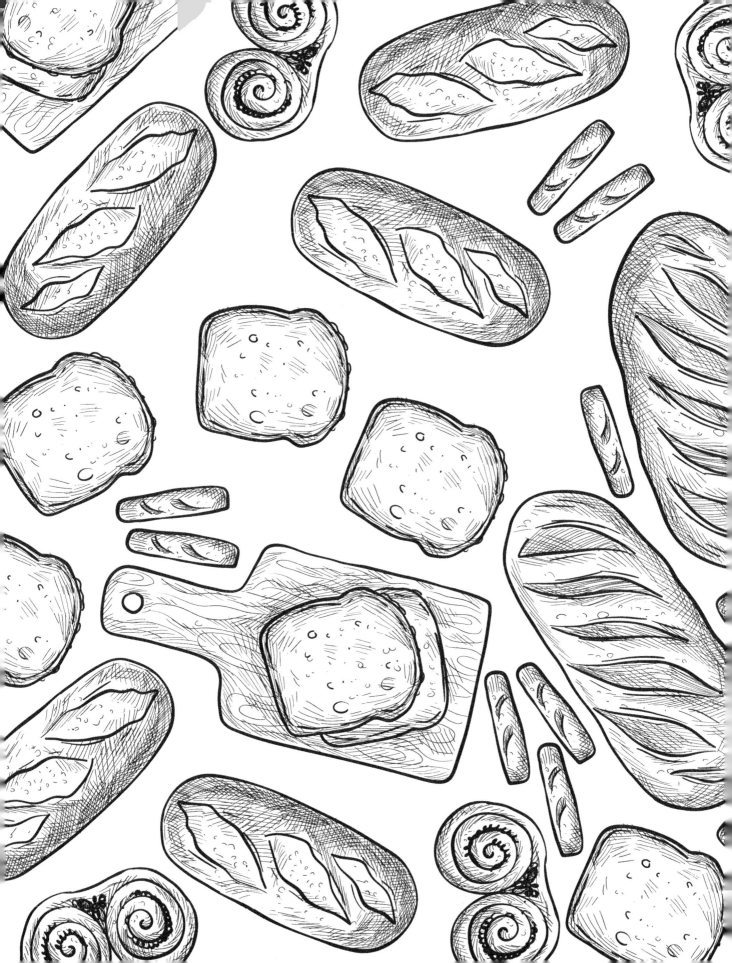

"...Give us today our daily bread."

Matthew 6:11

Bread Recipes

Flourless Nut & Seed Bread

Servings: 4 | Amount per Serving: 150g or 5 oz.
Preparation Time: 10 minutes | Cooking Time: 1 hour& 10 minutes

INGREDIENTS:

- 1.7 oz. chia seeds
- 1.7 oz. poppy seeds
- 2 tbsp. flax seeds
- 2.5 oz. flax meal
- 1.7 oz. sesame seeds
- 1.7 oz. pumpkin seeds
- 1.7 oz. walnuts
- 1.7 oz. mixed nuts (pecan + Brazil + almond)
- ½ cup (2.2 oz.) oats
- 2 tbsp. olive oil
- 3/4 cup (180 ml) luke warm water
- Salt to taste

NUTRITIONAL INFORMATION:
Energy (calories): 591kcal
Carbohydrates: 26.26 g
Protein: 17.44g
Fats: 52.17 g
Fiber: 15.4g

DIRECTIONS:

Preheat the oven to 340°F. Line a 9x5 inch loaf pan with parchment paper. In the meantime, in a wide bowl, add in the chia seeds, flax meal and flax seeds. Add lukewarm water and give everything a mix. Let this rest for 5 minutes. The seeds will absorb moisture and become gel-like. Next, add in the remaining ingredients and mix everything nicely. Make sure to check the bottom of the bowl, as dry ingredients may remain in the bottom. Once mixed, pour the batter in the prepared loaf pan. Flatten the top with the back of a spatula. Bake in a preheated oven for 1 hour. After 1 hour increase the temperature to 360°F, bake again for 10 minutes until it starts leaving the edges. Remove and let it cool completely in the loaf pan itself on a wire rack. Cut the slices when cooled completely. **Enjoy!**

Gluten Free Quinoa + Chia Bread

Servings: 4 | Amount per Serving: 100g or 3.5 oz.
Preparation Time: 10 minutes | Cooking Time: 1 ½ hour

INGREDIENTS:

- 10 ½ oz. quinoa seed, whole uncooked
- 2 oz. (¼ cup) chia seed, whole
- 1 cup water
- ½ lemon, juiced
- 2 fl. oz. olive oil
- ½ tsp. baking soda
- ½ tsp. sea salt

NUTRITIONAL INFORMATION:
Energy (calories): 476kcal
Carbohydrates: 51.49 g
Protein: 13.04 g
Fat: 25.07 g
Fiber 6.9g

DIRECTIONS:

Soak quinoa in plenty of cold water overnight in the fridge. Soak chia seed in ½ cup water until gel like. Preheat oven to 160°C / 320°F. Drain and rinse the quinoa. Place the quinoa into a food processor. Add chia gel, ½ cup of water, olive oil, baking soda, sea salt and lemon juice. Mix in a food processor for 3 minutes. The bread mix should resemble a batter consistency with some whole quinoa still left in the mix. Spoon into a loaf tin lined with oiled parchment paper. Bake for 1 ½ hours until firm to touch. Remove from the oven and cool for 30 minutes in the tin, then remove from the tin and cool completely on a rack. The bread should be slightly moist in the middle and crisp on the outside. Cool completely before eating. **Serve and enjoy!**

Golden Seed Bread

Servings: 4 to 8 slices | Amount per Serving: 90 g or 3 oz.
Preparation Time: 10 minute | Cooking Time: 1 hour

INGREDIENTS:

NUTRITIONAL INFORMATION:
Energy (calories): 591kcal
Carbohydrates: 26.26 g
Protein: 17.44g
Fats: 52.17 g
Fiber: 15.4g

- 1 ½ cups (130g) of certified gluten-free rolled/old fashioned oats, divided
- 2 Tbsp. avocado or olive oil or coconut oil
- 2 oz. pumpkin seeds, hulled
- 2 oz. sunflower seeds, hulled
- 3 oz. walnuts or pecans, chopped
- 1 oz. chia seeds
- 1 tsp. fine salt
- 2 tsp. lemon juice
- ½ tsp. baking soda
- 3/4 cup (180ml) almond milk
- 2 oz. flax seed, golden, ground

DIRECTIONS:

Grease and line a 9 x 5 inch loaf pan with parchment paper. Set aside. Take half the oats and put in a food processor or blender to make flour. Process/blend until flour-like then put into a large mixing bowl. Add all of the nuts and seeds, the unprocessed oats, salt and baking soda. Mix so they are combined. Next, add the oil, lemon and milk to the bowl. Stir to form a thick batter, then spoon into the lined loaf pan and pack it down. Preheat oven to 350 °F. Let the loaf rest in the pan while the oven preheats so that the flax and chia seeds absorb the moisture and bind everything together. Once the oven is to temperature bake the loaf on the middle shelf for 60 to 65 minutes or until a toothpick inserted into the middle comes out clean. Leave to cool in the pan for 5 minutes then gently remove and place on a cooling rack. Carefully remove the parchment paper and leave until completely cool before slicing or storing.

Note: *For nut-free version, you can replace the walnuts with pumpkin & sunflower seeds or hemp and sesame seeds.*

Red Lentil Flatbread

Servings: 4 | Amount per Serving: 100g g or 3.5 oz.
Preparation Time: 5 minutes | Cooking Time: 10 minutes

INGREDIENTS:

NUTRITIONAL INFORMATION:
Energy (calories): 591kcal
Carbohydrates: 26.26 g
Protein: 17.44g
Fats: 52.17 g
Fiber: 15.4g

- 1 cup (200 g) red lentils, uncooked, pre-soaked
- 2 cups (475 ml) water
- Salt & pepper, spices (optional)

DIRECTIONS:

Soak lentils in the water for 3 hours. Place in a high-speed blender. Blend it until creamy. Transfer to a bowl, add salt and pepper (if using) and combine with a whisk. Let the batter sit for 2-3 minutes so the lentils absorb some of the water and it becomes thicker. Heat up a non-stick frying pan. Ladle 1/3 cup of the batter and spread it as making pancakes. Cook 2-3 minutes over medium heat, then flip over and cook 1-2 minutes on the other side. Serve.

Note: *You can use similar to pancakes, wraps or crepes.*

Pumpkin Oat Banana Bread

Servings: 4 | Amount per Serving: 180g or 6 oz. or 2 slices
Preparation Time: 10 minutes | Cooking Time: 50 minutes

INGREDIENTS:

For the Flax Eggs
- 1 ½ Tbsp. (10 g) flaxseed meal
- 4 Tbsp. (60 ml) water

For the Bread:
- ¼ cup olive oil
- 1 cup pumpkin puree
- 1 banana, mashed
- ½ tsp. sea salt
- 2 tsp. baking soda
- ½ tsp. cinnamon, ground
- 1 tsp. pumpkin pie spice
- ½ cup water
- 1 cup gluten-free rolled oats
- 1 cup almond meal, ground from raw almonds
- 3 Tbsp. raw pecans

NUTRITIONAL INFORMATION:
Energy (calories): 591kcal
Carbohydrates: 26.26 g
Protein: 17.44g
Fats: 52.17 g
Fiber: 15.4g

DIRECTIONS:

Prepare flax eggs in a large mixing bowl by mixing the flax meal and water. Let it rest. Preheat oven to 375 degrees F (190 C). Prepare loaf pan by lining with oiled parchment paper. To flax eggs, add pumpkin, mashed banana and olive oil and whisk to combine. Next, add baking soda, salt, cinnamon, and pumpkin pie spice and whisk. Add water and whisk again. Add oats, almond meal and stir. If it appears too wet, add in another couple Tbsp. of oats. It should be semi-thick and pourable. Scoop into loaf pan and top with raw pecans. Bake for 40-45 minutes or until deep golden brown and a toothpick inserted into the center comes out clean. Remove from oven, let set in pan for at least 20 minutes and then gently transfer to a plate to cool. Let cool completely before slicing, preferably 2 hours. Otherwise, it can be a bit crumbly. **When cool, slice gently and enjoy.**

Potato Wrap

Servings: 4 | Amount per serving: 140g or 4.6 oz.
Preparation Time: 10 minutes | Cooking Time: 20 minutes

INGREDIENTS:

- 1 sweet potato
- 1 Yukon gold potato
- 1/2 cup oat flour (plus more for dusting)
- A pinch of salt

NUTRITIONAL INFORMATION:
Energy (calories): 184kcal
Carbohydrates: 24.98 g
Protein: 6.78g
Fat: 7.37 g
Fiber 3.9g

DIRECTIONS:

Peel, cook and mash potatoes. Let them cool, add flour and salt. Roll out into a log and divide into 4 equal portions. Flatten each portion into a biscuit shape dusting both sides with oat flour. Heat a non-stick pan or griddle to med-high heat. Roll each biscuit shape into a tortilla, generously dusting with flour as needed. Lay a tortilla into the hot pan and flip after 30-45 seconds. Continue flipping every 30 seconds or so until done. Cover with a towel and keep warm until used.

"But I am like a green olive tree in the
house of God. I trust in the steadfast
love of God forever and ever."

Psalm 52:8

Dips, Dressings & Sauces

Homemade BBQ Sauce

Servings: 4 | Amount per Serving: 120g or 4 oz.
Preparation Time: 5 minutes | Cooking Time: 1 hour

INGREDIENTS:

- 6 oz. tomato paste, can
- 1/3 cup apple cider vinegar
- 3 Tbsp. white wine vinegar
- 1/2 cup water (or more if too thick)
- 2 Tbsp. Worcestershire sauce
- 2 tsp. chili powder
- 1/2 tsp. adobo sauce or chipotle pepper
- 1/4 onion, grated
- 1 garlic clove, grated
- 1 tsp. salt
- 1/4 tsp. cinnamon
- 1/2 tsp. black pepper, ground
- 1-2 dates to sweeten (optional)

NUTRITIONAL INFORMATION:

Energy (calories): 56kcal
Carbohydrates: 11.66 g
Protein: 2.18 g
Fat: 0.42 g
Fiber 2.5g

DIRECTIONS:

Combine all of the ingredients in a medium saucepan over medium-high heat. Bring the mixture to a boil and then reduce the heat and let simmer on low, uncovered, for about an hour, until thick.

Aquafaba Vegan Mayonnaise

Servings: 4 | Amount per Serving: 40g or 1.3 oz.
Preparation Time: 5 minutes

INGREDIENTS:

- 1 tbsp. avocado oil or grapeseed oil
- ½ Tbsp. aquafaba, from canned chickpeas
- ½ Tbsp. Dijon mustard
- ½ Tbsp. apple cider vinegar
- ½ tsp. salt
- Pinch cayenne pepper, optional

NUTRITIONAL INFORMATION:

Energy (calories): 247kcal
Carbohydrates: 0.89 g
Protein: 0.35g
Fat: 27.42 g
Fiber 0.3g

DIRECTIONS:

Aquafaba is the liquid you drain from canned chickpeas. Add the aquafaba, Dijon mustard, vinegar, salt and pepper to mixing bowl and then pour in the oil. Let the ingredients sit for a few seconds. Insert your immersion blender and push it all the way down until it makes full contact with the bottom of the bowl. Blend for about 20 seconds until completely mixed.

Pico de Gallo

Servings: 2 | Preparation Time: 10 minutes

INGREDIENTS:

- 4 plum tomatoes, chopped
- 1/4 cup red onion, chopped
- 2 tbsp. fresh cilantro, chopped
- 1 small jalapeño pepper, chopped, seeds removed
- 1/2 tbsp. fresh lime juice.

DIRECTIONS:

Mix all the ingredient together. Refrigerate and serve cold.

Spinach Avocado dip

Servings: 4 | Amount per Serving: : 90g or 3.1 oz.
Preparation Time: 5 minutes

INGREDIENTS:

- 1 avocado, mashed
- 1 cup spinach, fresh
- 1 clove garlic, crushed
- 1 Tbsp. lime juice
- 2 Tbsp. olive or grapeseed oil
- ¼ tsp. sea salt
- 5cherry tomatoes, diced
- 1 Tbsp. fresh coriander

NUTRITIONAL INFORMATION:
Energy (calories): 148kcal
Carbohydrates: 5.96 g
Protein: 1.48g
Fats: 14.25 g
Fiber: 3.8g

DIRECTIONS:

Peel, and pit avocado. Blanch spinach in boiling water for 2 minutes, drain, and let it cool a bit. Add the avocados, garlic, spinach, coriander, lime juice, salt, oil, and coriander to your food processor and pulse till mixture becomes smooth. Transfer the mixture to a bowl and add diced cherry tomatoes. Put the mixture in your refrigerator and refrigerate for about 30 minutes. Adjust to taste.

Roasted Bell Pepper Humus

Servings: 4 | Amount per Serving: : 140g or 4.6 oz.
Preparation Time: 10 minutes

INGREDIENTS:

- 3/4 cup roasted red peppers, chopped
- 1 (15 oz.) can chickpeas or 1 ½ cups (250 grams) cooked chickpeas
- 1/4 cup (60 ml) fresh lemon juice
- 1/4 cup (60 ml) tahini
- 1 garlic clove, minced
- 2 Tbsp. extra virgin olive oil, plus more for serving
- 1/2 tsp. cumin, ground
- Pinch cayenne pepper (optional)
- Salt to taste

NUTRITIONAL INFORMATION:
Energy (calories): 288kcal
Carbohydrates: 27.06 g
Protein: 9.8g
Fat: 17 g
Fiber 7.7g

DIRECTIONS:

Put all ingredients in a blender or food processer and blend until smooth. Adjust consistency by adding water if necessary.

Cannellini Mayo Dressing

Servings: 4 | Amount per serving: 40g or 1.4 oz. | Preparation Time: 3 minutes

INGREDIENTS:

- 2 - 15 oz. cans of cannellini beans, drained
- 2 tsp. Dijon mustard
- 4 tbsp. of lemon juice - start with 1 tsp., add more if desired
- 3 tsp. salt
- ½ tsp. onion powder
- ½ tsp. garlic powder
- ½ cup of water

DIRECTIONS:

Put all ingredients in mixing bowl, whisk until smooth with a fork or whisk. *Note: For nutritional info, see Green Bean Salad recipe.*

Olive Tapenade

Yield: 2 cups

INGREDIENTS:

- 1 cup pitted black olives, such as Niçoise or oil-cured olives
- ½ cup green olives
- 1 Tbsp. drained capers
- 2 drained oil-packed anchovy fillets (optional)
- 2 cloves garlic, crushed
- ½ tsp. basil
- 1 Tbsp. loosely packed fresh oregano, marjoram, or thyme leaves
- 1 tsp. Dijon mustard
- 1 tsp. fresh juice from 1 lemon
- 1 scallion, chopped
- Extra-virgin olive oil, as needed
- Kosher salt and freshly ground black pepper, if needed

DIRECTIONS:

Combine all ingredients, except olive oil in the food processor or blender. With the processor running, drizzle in just enough olive oil to loosen to a spreadable paste, about 2 Tbsp. Season with salt and pepper only if needed.

Rosemary Walnut Pâté

Yield: 2 cups

INGREDIENTS:

- 1 cup walnuts
- 1 tbsp. olive oil
- 1 yellow onion, chopped
- 2 cloves garlic, minced
- 2 cups button mushrooms, sliced
- ½ cup parsley, chopped
- 2 tbsp. fresh rosemary, chopped
- 1 tsp. salt
- ½ tsp. pepper

NUTRITIONAL INFORMATION:

Energy (calories): 176kcal

Carbohydrates: 12.29 g

Protein: 5.28g

Fats: 13.55 g

Fibers: 5g

DIRECTIONS:

Place all ingredients in a food processor or blender and blend until smooth.

Chipotle Sauce

Servings: 4 | Amount per serving: 40g or 1.4 oz. | Preparation Time: 3 minutes

INGREDIENTS:

- ½ cup Creamy Mayo Dressing (see recipe above)
- 2 Tbsp. lime juice (to taste)
- ¼ tsp. salt, more to taste
- ¼ tsp. chipotle powder
- 1 tsp. smoked paprika
- ½ tsp. chili powder
- 1 Tbsp. water

DIRECTIONS:

Put all ingredients in mixing bowl, whisk until smooth with a fork or whisk.

Baba Ganesh Eggplant Dip

Servings: 4 | Amount per Serving: 360 g or 12 oz.
Preparation Time: 10 minutes | Cooking Time: 45 minutes

INGREDIENTS:

- 2 lbs. globe eggplant
- 3 tbsp. extra virgin olive oil
- 2-3 tbsp. tahini
- 2 garlic cloves, finely chopped
- ½ tsp. cumin, ground

- 1 lemon, juiced
- Salt and pepper to taste
- cayenne pepper (optional)
- 1 tbsp. parsley, chopped
- handful walnuts, chopped to garnish

DIRECTIONS:

Preheat oven to 400°F. Poke the eggplants in several places with the tines of a fork. Cut the eggplants in half lengthwise and brush the cut sides lightly with olive oil (about 1 tbsp.). Place on a baking sheet, cut side down, and roast until very tender, about 35-40 minutes. Remove from oven and allow to cool for 15 minutes. Scoop the eggplant flesh into a large bowl and mash well with a fork. Add all remaining ingredients. Mash well. Let the Baba Ganesh cool to room temperature, then season to taste with additional lemon juice, salt, and cayenne. If you want, swirl a little olive oil on the top. Sprinkle with fresh chopped parsley and chopped walnuts.

Avocado Dressing

INGREDIENTS:

- 1 avocado, peeled, seeded
- ½ cup (80 ml) water or veggie nut milk
- 2 tbsp. extra virgin olive oil
- 1 tbsp. lime juice

- 1 tsp. chili powder
- 1/4 tsp. cumin
- Salt and freshly ground black pepper to taste

DIRECTIONS:

Pit and peel avocado, add water, olive oil, lime juice, chili powder, cumin, a pinch of salt and freshly ground black pepper and process with a food processor or an immersion blender until smooth.

"In the morning, Lord, you hear my voice; in the morning I lay my requests before you and wait expectantly."

Psalm 5:3

Breakfast Recipes

SMOOTHIES

Ireland Apple Berry Smoothie

Servings: 4 | Amount per Serving: 450g or 15.9 oz.
Preparation Time: 5 minutes

INGREDIENTS:

- 2 cup mixed greens
- 4 cups spinach, baby leaves, organic
- 4 cups mixed berries
- 2 apples, cored
- 1 cup blueberry, frozen
- 5 Tbsp. flaxseed, organic powder
- 2 cups orange juice, raw, homemade

NUTRITIONAL INFORMATION:
Energy (calories): 311kcal
Carbohydrates: 66.12 g
Protein: 5.83g
Fats: 5.61 g
Fibers: 11.3g

DIRECTIONS:

Blend and enjoy!

Love Berry Kiwi Smoothie

Servings: 4 | Amount per Serving: 480 g or 16 oz.
Preparation Time: 5 minutes

INGREDIENTS:

- 4 apples, cored
- 2 cups blueberries, frozen
- 2 cups cantaloupe, frozen chunks
- 4 handful spinach or arugula
- 4 fresh kiwi fruit, peeled
- 6 tbsp. flaxseed, ground
- ½ cup water

DIRECTIONS:

Blend and enjoy!

Ola Mango Peach Smoothie

Servings: 4 | Amount per Serving: 300g
Preparation Time: 5 minutes

INGREDIENTS:

- 2 cups Romaine lettuce
- 4 cups spinach, baby leaves, organic, raw.
- 2 cups frozen mango-peach mix
- 1 cup grapes, seedless.
- 2 cups strawberries, fresh or frozen
- 1 cup blueberries, fresh or frozen
- 5 tbsp. flaxseed, organic powder

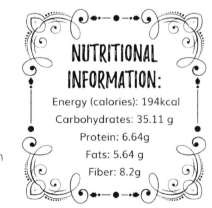

NUTRITIONAL INFORMATION:
Energy (calories): 194kcal
Carbohydrates: 35.11 g
Protein: 6.64g
Fats: 5.64 g
Fiber: 8.2g

DIRECTIONS: Blend and enjoy!

Viva Red Smoothie

Servings: 4 | Amount per Serving: 320g or 10.6 oz.
Preparation Time: 5 minutes

INGREDIENTS:

- 3 bananas, peeled
- 2 cups blueberries, frozen
- 4 cups arugula
- 2 cups Almond milk
- 6 tbsp. flaxseed, ground

DIRECTIONS:

Blend and enjoy!

Energy Green Bliss Smoothie

Servings: 4 | Amount per serving: 450g or 15 oz.
Preparation Time: 5 minutes

INGREDIENTS:

- 2 cups almond milk, unsweetened
- 4 cup frozen pineapple chunks
- 2 cup frozen mango chunks
- 2 banana, sliced
- 8 tbsp. flaked coconut, unsweetened
- 4 tbsp. flax meal or seeds
- 4 cups baby spinach

DIRECTIONS:

Place all ingredients in a blender & blend until smooth. Enjoy!

Glowing Pink Smoothie

Servings: 4 | Amount per serving: 480g or 16 oz.
Preparation Time: 10 minutes

INGREDIENTS:

- 4 juicy tangerines, peeled and broken into segments
- 3 small beet, peeled and chopped
- 2 cups red berries or raspberries or strawberries
- 2 ripe bananas, preferably frozen
- 3 tbsp. raw or roasted almond butter
- 4 tbsp. chia seeds
- 3 cups almond milk, unsweetened
- 2 tsp. cinnamon
- Pinch fine sea salt (omit if using salted almond butter)

DIRECTIONS:

Place all ingredients in a blender and blend until smooth. Enjoy!

Ombré Pineapple Mango

Servings: 4 | Amount per Serving: 510g or 17 oz.
Preparation Time: 5 minutes

INGREDIENTS:

- 4 cups fresh spinach
- 3 cups water
- 2 cups pineapple, frozen
- 2 cups mango, frozen
- 3 bananas
- 3 Tbsp. ground flaxseeds

DIRECTIONS:

Place all ingredients in a blender and blend until smooth. Enjoy!

NUTRITIONAL INFORMATION:

Energy (calories): 278kcal

Carbohydrates: 63.18 g

Protein: 5.94g

Fats: 3.29 g

Fiber: 7.2g

Delicious Strawberry Oatmeal

Servings: 4 | Amount per Serving: 300g or 10 oz.
Preparation Time: 5 minutes

INGREDIENTS:

- 2 cups almond milk
- 1 cup rolled oats
- 2 cups strawberries, frozen
- 2 bananas, broken into chunks
- 1/2 cup raisins

DIRECTIONS:

blend all in a blender and serve immediately.

NUTRITIONAL INFORMATION:

Energy (calories): 278kcal

Carbohydrates: 63.18 g

Protein: 5.94g

Fats: 3.29 g

Fiber: 7.2g

Berry Chia Breakfast Bowl

Servings: 4 | Amount per serving: 380 g or 12.6 oz.
Preparation Time: 15 minutes | Cooking Time: 15 minutes

NUTRITIONAL INFORMATION:
Energy (calories): 315 kcal
Carbohydrates: 52.43 g
Protein: 7.37 g
Fats: 10.87 g
Fiber: 11.8 g

INGREDIENTS:

- 8 pitted dates
- 1 ½ cups almond milk
- 4 tbsp. blanched almonds or raw cashews
- 4 tsp. frozen orange juice concentrate
- 1 tsp. vanilla
- 1 pinch salt
- 4 cups sliced or diced, strawberries, divided
- 3/4 cup chia seed
- 1 ½ cup fresh blueberries
- 2 small bananas, sliced (optional)

DIRECTIONS:

Place dates, almond milk, nuts, orange juice concentrate, vanilla, salt, and 1 cup strawberries in blender and blend until smooth. Transfer blender mixture to medium bowl and stir in chia seed. Place in refrigerator for at least 2 hours, or overnight. Stir in blueberries, remaining strawberries (sliced), and sliced bananas just before serving.

Homemade Granola

Servings: 4 | Amount per serving: 80g or 2.6 oz.
Preparation Time: 5 minutes | Cooking Time: 10 minutes

INGREDIENTS:

- 1 cup rolled oats
- ¼ cup raw pecans chopped
- ¼ cup pumpkin seeds
- ¼ cup almond butter
- ½ tsp. vanilla extract
- 1 Tbsp. chia seeds
- ¼ cup dried sugar-free cranberries

DIRECTIONS:

Preheat oven to 300°F. Combine oats, chopped nuts, pumpkin seeds, chia seeds, and cranberries. Pour almond butter and vanilla extract over oat mixture. Stir to combine until oats are wet. Spread mixture evenly over a cookie sheet. Place in oven and toast for 8-10 minutes. Be careful not to burn the oats.

Take out of the oven and allow to cool completely before storing granola in an air tight container.
Notes: Add your own favorite sugar-free dried fruit, and raw nuts. If oat mixture needs more moisture add 1 Tbsp. of almond butter until all oats are wet.

Smoothie Bowl with Berries & Granola

Servings: 4 | Amount per Serving: 430 g or 14.3 oz.
Preparation Time: 10 minutes

INGREDIENTS:

- 3 cups almond milk
- 2 cups blueberries, frozen
- 2 cups peaches, mango, or pineapple, frozen
- 2 ripe bananas
- 1 cup fresh spinach
- 4 tbsp. chia seeds, pre-soaked
- 2 tbsp. flax seeds
- 1 tsp. Vanilla extract (optional)
- 1/2 cup granola, plus more if desired
- Additional toppings: fresh fruit, nuts

NUTRITIONAL INFORMATION:
Energy (calories): 365 kcal
Carbohydrates: 54.64 g
Protein: 8.99 g
Fats: 14.24 g
Fiber: 10.8 g

DIRECTIONS:

In a blender, combine the almond milk, frozen blueberries, frozen peaches, banana, spinach, chia seeds, flax seeds and a dash of vanilla extract if desired. Purée until smooth, about 1 minute. The smoothie should be thick, so if needed, add more frozen fruit until desired consistency is reached. Pour into a bowl and top with granola and fresh fruit. Eat immediately.

OATMEAL

Cinnamon Old Fashion Oatmeal

Servings: 4 | Amount per Serving: 360g or 12 oz.
Preparation Time: 5 minutes | Cooking Time: 15 minutes

INGREDIENTS:

- 3 cups water
- 1 tbsp. cinnamon
- 2 cups old-fashioned rolled oats
- 4 dates
- 1 oz. (14 halves) walnuts
- 1 cup strawberry, sliced
- 2 bananas, sliced

DIRECTIONS:

In a medium saucepan, bring 2 cups water and cinnamon to a boil. Reduce the heat and add the oatmeal. Once it's simmering, turn off the heat, cover and let stand 15 minutes, until thick and creamy. Place the mixture in a bowl and add the rest of the listed ingredients.

Creamy Pumpkin Oats with Blueberries & Toasted Almonds

Servings: 4 | Amount per serving: 430g or 10.6oz.
Preparation Time: 5 minutes

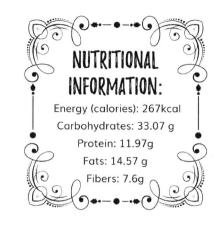

NUTRITIONAL INFORMATION:
Energy (calories): 267kcal
Carbohydrates: 33.07 g
Protein: 11.97g
Fats: 14.57 g
Fibers: 7.6g

INGREDIENTS:

- 2 cups rolled oats
- 2 cups almond milk, unsweetened
- 2 cups water
- pinch salt
- 1 tsp. of flaxseed meal
- ½ tsp. cinnamon
- 8 Tbsp. pumpkin puree
- ¼ tsp. pumpkin spice
- 1 ½ cups of blueberries (fresh or frozen)
- ¼ cup toasted almonds (crushed)

DIRECTIONS:

Bring the almond milk and water to a boil in a small saucepan. Add oats and salt and reduce heat to medium. Stirring occasionally, cook for 2 minutes and then add pumpkin. Cook for 3-4 minutes more or until creamy, being careful to stir often. In the meantime, toast almonds in a skillet over medium-high heat until dark brown on all sides. When ready, remove oats from heat and add flaxseed, cinnamon, pumpkin spice and stir. Microwave blueberries in your serving dish until thawed (if frozen) and warm. Add blueberries, top with oats and almonds and enjoy.

Granola with Fruits and Almond Milk

Servings: 4 | Amount per Serving: 260g or 8.6 oz. | Preparation Time: 5 minutes

INGREDIENTS:

Homemade prepared granola
- 1 cup fresh blueberries
- 1 cup fresh raspberries
- 2 bananas, sliced
- 2 tbsp. almonds, sliced
- 2 cups almond milk

DIRECTIONS:

Divide granola into 4 bowls. Top with fruit and milk.

Banana Porridge

Servings: 4 | Amount per serving: 340 g or 11.3 oz.
Preparation Time: 5 minutes | Cooking Time: 15 minutes

INGREDIENTS:

- 2 cups (320g) rolled oats
- 5 cups water
- 1 tsp. salt
- 4 bananas, sliced
- 2 tbsp. cinnamon, ground
- 4 tbsp. raspberries

NUTRITIONAL INFORMATION:

Energy (calories): 433 kcal

Carbohydrates: 85.52 g

Protein: 14.75 g

Fats: 5.84 g

Fiber: 13.9 g

DIRECTIONS:

In a saucepan, combine the oats, water, salt, bananas and cinnamon. Bring to a boil, then reduce heat to low, and simmer until the liquid has been absorbed, stirring frequently. Pour into bowls, and top each with berries.

Chia-Papaya Pudding

Servings: 4 | Amount per Serving: 260 g or 8.6 oz.
Preparation Time: 5 minutes

INGREDIENTS:

- 9 tbsp. chia seeds
- 3 cups almond milk
- 1 papaya
- 6 dried prunes
- 1 tbsp. cinnamon

NUTRITIONAL INFORMATION:

Energy (calories): 311kcal

Carbohydrates: 50.46 g

Protein: 7.75g

Fats: 10.79g

Fiber: 12.g

DIRECTIONS:

Mix together chia seeds, milk, and cinnamon. Keep stirring for couple of minutes until chia seeds start to form gel like texture. Transfer into small jar and place in the fridge for at least 3-4 hours (ideally overnight). In a blender, mix together papaya, dried prunes and a bit of water until smooth. Using tall glass or jar, fill it up with papaya mousse and chia layers. Serve chilled.

Barley Pudding with Fruits & Nuts

Servings: 4 | Amount per Serving: 290g or 10 oz.
Preparation Time: 5 minutes | Cooking Time: 10 minutes

INGREDIENTS:

- 4 oz. whole barley, pre-soaked
- 2 tsp. vegan butter
- 1 ½ cups boiling water
- ½ tsp. cinnamon, ground
- 2 ½ oz. walnut halves
- 1 cup blueberries
- 4 tbsp. pomegranate seeds, fresh
- 4 small dates or figs, quartered
- 1 cup almond milk, to serve
- banana (optional)

DIRECTIONS:

Boil the barley in a large pot. Cook until soft. Drain water. Add milk and dates and simmer until hot. Add cinnamon and decorate with the walnuts, blueberries, pomegranate seeds and figs (if using), or with other toppings of your choice. Taste and adjust cinnamon accordingly. Add milk if too thick. If too thin, add ground flaxseed or mashed banana.

Fruit Breakfast Pudding

Servings: 4 | Amount per Serving: 290 g or 9.6 oz.
Preparation Time: 5 minutes

INGREDIENTS:

- 4 cups mixed berries, frozen
- 4 bananas, sliced, frozen
- 10 tbsp. almond milk
- 4 tbsp. flaxseeds
- 2 tsp. cinnamon

DIRECTIONS:

Add frozen berries and banana to a blender and blend on low until small bits remain. Add almond milk flaxseeds and cinnamon and blend on low again, scraping down sides as needed, until the mixture reaches a soft serve consistency. Serve.

Creamy Breakfast Rice Pudding

Servings: 4 | Amount per serving: 430g or 14.3 oz.
Preparation Time: 5 minutes | Cooking Time: 10 minutes

INGREDIENTS:

- 4 cups precooked brown rice loosely packed (reserve 1 cup)
- 2 cup non-dairy milk of your choice
- 3 ripe bananas
- 4 dried prunes
- 1 tsp. cinnamon
- 2 Tbsp. of nut or seed butter (ex: cashew, almond)
- Few pinches nutmeg
- 1/4 tsp. sea salt
- Grated orange or lemon zest - optional

NUTRITIONAL INFORMATION:
Energy (calories): 427kcal
Carbohydrates: 80.74 g
Protein: 9.18g
Fats: 8.97 g
Fibers: 7.2g

DIRECTIONS:

In a small saucepan, add 3 cups of the cooked rice (rough measure), and the remaining ingredients starting with 3/4 cup of milk. Puree the mixture using a hand blender (alternatively, you can puree in a blender before adding to the saucepan. Add the remaining cup of rice, and turn heat to medium-low. Let the mixture thicken and warm for several minutes. Add the remaining milk if desired to thin. Taste, and adjust with orange/lemon zest if desired, and stirring through add-ins if you like! Serve.

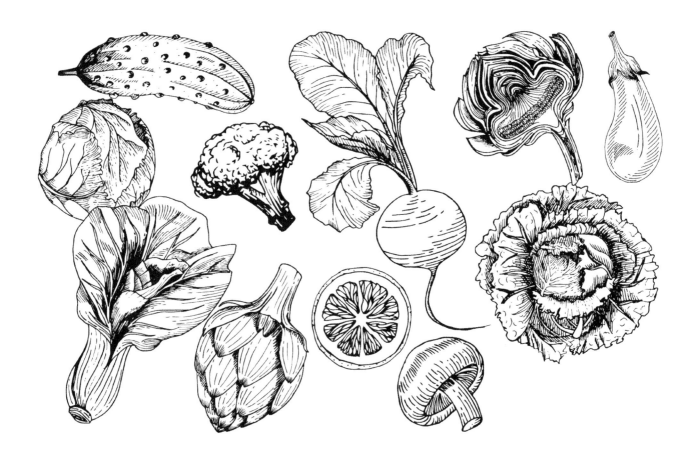

Sweet Potato toast with Baba Ganesh (Eggplant Dip)

Servings: 4 | Amount per serving: 360 g or 12 oz.
Preparation Time: 10 minutes | Cooking Time: 45 minutes

INGREDIENTS:

For Sweet Potato
- 1 large sweet potato
- 1 tsp. oil
- Salt and pepper to taste

For Eggplant Dip:
- 2 lbs. globe eggplant
- 3 tbsp. extra virgin olive oil
- 2-3 tbsp. tahini
- 2 garlic cloves, finely chopped
- ½ tsp. cumin, ground
- 1 lemon, juiced
- Salt and pepper to taste
- Cayenne pepper (optional)
- 1 tbsp. parsley, chopped

DIRECTIONS:

Preheat oven to 400°F. Poke the eggplants in several places with the tines of a fork. Cut the eggplants in half lengthwise and brush the cut sides lightly with olive oil (about 1 tbsp.).

For Eggplant Dip: Place on a baking sheet, cut side down, and roast until very tender, about 35-40 minutes. Remove from oven and allow to cool for 15 minutes. Scoop the eggplant flesh into a large bowl and mash well with a fork. Add all ingredients for dip. Mash well. Let the Baba Ganesh to cool to room temperature, then season to taste with additional lemon juice, salt, and cayenne. If you want, swirl a little olive oil on the top. Sprinkle with fresh chopped parsley. Serve with Sweet potato toast.

For Sweet Potato: Slice the ends of the sweet potato off, then cut it lengthwise into 1/2-inch thick slices. Arrange the slices in a single layer on an oiled baking sheet. Bake until the slices are tender and easily pierced with a fork, about 20 minutes. Serve warm with your favorite toast toppings.

Oat Pancakes with Spread of Dried Dates & Walnuts

Servings: 4 | Amount per Serving: 300g or 10 oz.
Preparation Time: 10 minutes | Cooking Time: 10 minutes

NUTRITIONAL INFORMATION:
Energy (calories): 336 kcal
Carbohydrates: 44.16 g
Protein: 8.17g
Fats: 15.66 g
Fiber: 5.5g

INGREDIENTS:

- 2 cups (180 g) oat flour (simply process oats in a blender)
- 1 ½ cups (330 ml) almond milk
- 1 medium banana
- 2 tbsp. oil

For Spread:
- 6 oz. dried dates, previously soaked in water for 10 minutes and drained
- 5 oz. walnuts
- Zest 2 lemons
- 3 tsp. cinnamon
- 3 tbsp. water

DIRECTIONS:

In a bowl, mash the banana with a fork, add the other ingredients and stir with a whisk until just combined. Heat a little oil in a skillet over medium heat. Spoon some of the batter (I use one heaping ice cream scoop) into the hot skillet and cook the pancake on low to medium from both sides until golden brown.Repeat with the rest of batter (approx. 8 pancakes). Serve them with spread of dried dates & walnuts. For spread just put all ingredients in a blender and blend it until you get a nice smooth mass. Don't forget to soak the dates for 10 minutes, before blending them.

Sweet Potato Waffles with Banana-Strawberries Spread

Servings: 4
Amount per Serving: 400 g/14.1 oz. Makes 10-11 waffles
Preparation Time: 5 minutes | Cooking Time: 10 minutes

NUTRITIONAL INFORMATION:
Energy (calories): 493 kcal
Carbohydrates: 99.41 g
Protein: 11.95 g
Fats: 5.45 g
Fiber: 12 g

INGREDIENTS:

- 6 cups sweet potato, cooked or canned
- 4 cups oat flour
- 8 tsp. vanilla extract

For Banana-Strawberries Spread
- 6 bananas, fork smashed
- 2 cup strawberries, finely chopped
- ½ tsp. vanilla extract

DIRECTIONS:

Heat the waffle iron. Mix ingredients in a bowl and spoon batter onto the oiled waffle iron. Leave the lid down 5-8 minutes to make sure the waffles do not pull apart. Mix ingredients for Banana-Strawberries Spread and place on top of the waffle.

Apple Cake with Dried Prunes

Servings: 4 | Amount per serving: 140g or 4.6 oz.
Preparation Time: 10 minutes | Cooking Time: 25 minutes

INGREDIENTS:

- ½ cup almond milk
- 1 tbsp. applesauce
- ¼ tsp. apple cider vinegar
- 3 tbsp. neutral oil
- 1/4 tsp. vanilla extract
- A few drops almond extract
- 1 cup oats flour
- ½ tsp. baking soda
- 1 tsp. lemon juice
- 1 tsp. cinnamon or pumpkin pie spice
- 1/8 tsp. salt
- 4 dried prunes, soaked for 10 minutes and chopped
- 1 apple chopped medium

DIRECTIONS:

Line a pan with parchment with parchment hanging on the sides. Preheat the oven to 350° F (176 °C). In a bowl, mix in the wet ingredients for the cake, until is fully combined. Add oat flour, baking soda, cinnamon and salt. Fold into the wet until just about combined to make just slightly thick batter. Add chopped or diced apple and prunes to the batter and mix it in. Pour into the parchment lined pan and even it out. Bake for 20 to 25 minutes.

Collard Greens Banana Wrap

Servings: 4 | Amount per serving: 160g or 5.3 oz.
Preparation Time: 5 minutes

INGREDIENTS:

- 4 large collard greens leaves, rinsed and dried
- 6 tbsp. peanut butter, crunchy
- 4 bananas
- 4 tbsp. flaxseed meal
- Optional: sunflower seeds or shredded coconut or celery w/ nuts

NUTRITIONAL INFORMATION:

Energy (calories): 305kcal
Carbohydrates: 35.49 g
Protein: 8.65g
Fats: 17.08 g
Fiber: 7.2g

DIRECTIONS:

Flatten your collard greens and, with a knife, shave the stem down so it's easier to roll up. Alternatively, cut out the bottom portion that tends to be more rigid. Starting at the bottom about 1/4 of the way up smear on peanut butter, add flaxseed, banana and roll the whole thing up like a regular wrap, tucking the sides in as you near the top. Secure with a tooth pick and cut in half. Or, simply grasp in your hands and enjoy immediately!

Apple Tart with Nuts

Servings: 4 | Amount per Serving: 250g or 8.3 oz.
Preparation Time: 20 minutes

INGREDIENTS:

- 1 ½ cups (120g) walnuts, ground
- 1 cup almonds, ground
- ½ cup hazelnut, whole
- 3 apples
- 4 oz. dried dates, chopped
- 4 tbsp. freshly squeezed orange juice, plus more (if the "stuffing" is too firm)
- 1 tbsp. cinnamon

DIRECTIONS:

Mix a cup of walnuts in a blender and add one-third of dried dates. Add a tbsp. or two of orange juice and stir with hands until you get a thick mixture, but at the same time it needs to be soft enough so you can shape it. Shape the crust in the form of a cake. Cut half the apples in smaller dices, and rest into very thin slices. Mix the apples with cinnamon; add a few tbsp. of orange juice and rest of the dates. Line diced apples first, and then sliced apples over the crust. Sprinkle with ground almonds and whole hazelnuts.Let it stand a bit until apples soften. Serve.

Breakfast Baked Apples

Servings: 4 | Amount per Serving: 430g or 14.3oz.
Preparation Time: 10 minutes | Cooking Time: 35 minutes

INGREDIENTS:

- 2 cups old-fashioned rolled oats
- 3 cups of water
- 1 Tbsp. ground cinnamon
- 2 Tbsp. pecans, chopped
- 4 large baking apples, tops sliced and insides hollowed
- 2 Tbsp. dried cranberries

DIRECTIONS:

Preheat oven to 400°. In a medium saucepan over medium-low heat, combine oatmeal and water and stir occasionally until creamy. Stir in ground cinnamon and let cool slightly. Transfer apples to a glass baking dish and spoon in oatmeal. Bake until apples are soft and bubbly, about 35 minutes. Top oatmeal with cranberries and pecans and serve.

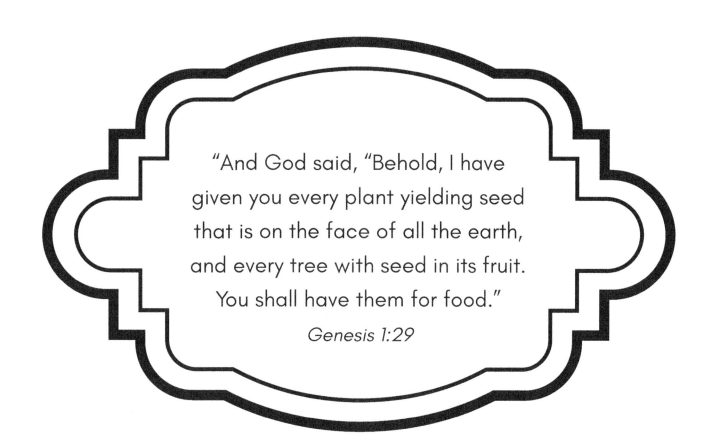

"And God said, "Behold, I have given you every plant yielding seed that is on the face of all the earth, and every tree with seed in its fruit. You shall have them for food."

Genesis 1:29

Salad Recipes

Greek Salad

Servings: 4 | Amount per serving: 240g or 8 oz.
Preparation Time: 10 minutes

INGREDIENTS:

- 2 (400g) cucumbers, sliced
- 4 (60g) scallions, chopped
- 4 (1 lbs.) tomatoes, ripe
- 2 (240g) green bell peppers, seeded, chopped
- 4 oz. Kalamata olives, pitted
- 4 Tbsp. of olive oil
- Salt and pepper to taste
- 2 Tbsp. dill, fresh chopped
- Garnish: chopped parsley

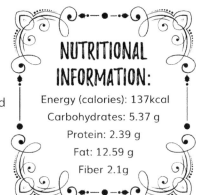

NUTRITIONAL INFORMATION:
Energy (calories): 200kcal
Carbohydrates: 9.81 g
Protein: 2.18 g
Fat: 8.22 g
Fiber 3.8g

DIRECTIONS:

Add all the ingredients in a bowl and toss gently. Garnish with parsley.

Watercress and Lettuce Salad with Seeds

Servings: 4 | Amount per serving: 110 g or 3.8oz.
Preparation Time: 10 minutes

INGREDIENTS:

- 4 cups (140g) watercress
- 3 cups (140g) lettuce, shredded
- 1 cup (110g) carrots, grated
- 3 Tbsp. of extra virgin olive oil
- 1 Tbsp. of lemon juice
- 2 Tbsp. sunflower seeds, roasted
- Salt to taste

NUTRITIONAL INFORMATION:
Energy (calories): 137kcal
Carbohydrates: 5.37 g
Protein: 2.39 g
Fat: 12.59 g
Fiber 2.1g

DIRECTIONS:

Add all the ingredients in a bowl and toss gently.
Garnish with roasted sunflower seeds.

Lettuce Radish Salad

Servings: 4 | Amount per serving: 70g or 2.3 oz.
Preparation Time: 10 minutes

INGREDIENTS:

- 2 cups Romaine lettuce, shredded
- 10 radishes, sliced
- 1 cucumber, sliced
- 4 scallions, chopped
- Salt and pepper to taste
- ½ cup fresh dill, chopped

Dressing:
- 2 Tbsp. lemon juice
- 3 Tbsp. olive oil

NUTRITIONAL INFORMATION:
Energy (calories): 102kcal
Carbohydrates: 2.84 g
Protein: 0.68 g
Fat: 10.26 g
Fiber 1.1g

DIRECTIONS:

Add all the ingredients in a bowl and mix thoroughly.

Cabbage Salad

Servings: 4 | Amount per Serving: 200g or 6.6 oz.
Preparation Time: 10 minutes

INGREDIENTS:

- 5 cups (350g) green cabbage, shredded
- 2 cups (140g red cabbage, shredded
- 1 cup (110g) carrot, shredded

Dressing:
- 1 Tbsp. of apple cider vinegar
- 3 Tbsp. oil olive oil
- 1 tsp. Dijon mustard
- 1 Tbsp. of water
- ½ tsp. salt

NUTRITIONAL INFORMATION:
Energy (calories): 154kcal
Carbohydrates: 14.22 g
Protein: 2.53g
Fat: 10.86 g
Fiber 4.1g

DIRECTIONS:

Shake dressing ingredients in a jar. Place salad ingredients in a large bowl. Pour over dressing, toss. Set aside 20 minutes - mound will reduce by almost half and become juicy! Serve.

Maria's Eggplant Salad

Servings: 6

INGREDIENTS:

- 2 Eggplant peeled and chopped into 1-2 -inch cubes
- 1-3 clove garlic, mashed (use garlic-press)
- 1 cup dill chopped
- 1 cup parsley chopped

- 4 roasted red bell peppers, sliced
- 5-6 olives
- 1 tbs. vinegar
- ¼ cup olive oil
- 4 scallions, chopped

For the Marinade
- 1 cup vinegar
- 2 tbs. salt
- 6 cups of water

DIRECTIONS:

Place water with vinegar and salt in large pot. Boil. Add the eggplant. Cover the pot with a lid and boil until the eggplant is tender. Remove the pot from the stove. Strain the liquid in a colander for a few minutes. Place the cooked eggplant in a bowl and mix scallions, garlic, dill, parsley, 5 tbsp. of olive oil and 3 minced, roasted red peppers. Taste and adjust as necessary. Refrigerate. Serve cold. Garnish with olives, 1 roasted red bell pepper and za'atar. Drizzle with olive oil (about two tablespoons).

Arugula Salad with Seeds

Servings: 4 | Amount per serving: 90g or 3 oz. | Preparation Time: 5 minutes

INGREDIENTS:

- 8 cups arugula
- 8 Tbsp. extra-virgin olive oil
- Freshly ground black pepper

- 4 Tbsp. of roasted sunflower seeds
- 4 Tbsp. lemon juice
- Kosher salt

DIRECTIONS:

Make dressing: In a medium bowl, whisk together olive oil and lemon juice, and then season with salt and pepper. Add arugula and then top with a spoonful of roasted sunflower seeds.

Spinach Mashed Potatoes Salad

Servings: 4 | Amount per Serving: 180g or 6 oz.

INGREDIENTS:

- 1 lb. of potatoes, cut into ½ inch cubes
- 2 Tbsp. almond vegan butter
- 3 Tbsp. almond milk, unsweetened
- 1 tsp. sea salt
- ½ tsp. black pepper, ground
- 1 tsp. olive oil
- 1 tsp. garlic, finely minced
- 6 oz. baby spinach leaves

NUTRITIONAL INFORMATION:

Energy (calories): 163kcal

Carbohydrates: 23.94 g

Protein: 5.45g

Fats: 6.08 g

Fiber: 4.4g

DIRECTIONS:

Into a large saucepan, add the cubed potatoes and enough water to cover by 1inch. Bring to a boil then reduce heat to low. Simmer until the potatoes are easily pierced with a fork, approximately 15 minutes. Drain potatoes in a colander then return to the saucepan.

Putting it all together: Into the pot with the potatoes, add the vegan butter, unsweetened almond milk, sea salt, and ground black pepper. Use a potato masher to mash to desired consistency. Add the cooked spinach. Stir everything together to combine. Adjust seasoning taste. Serve hot.

For the spinach: While the potatoes are simmering, add the olive oil to a medium-size skillet over medium-high heat. When the oil is hot, add the baby spinach leaves. Cook, stirring frequently until the leaves begin to wilt. Add the minced garlic then continue cooking an additional 1 minute. Remove cooked spinach to a cutting board. Rough chop and set aside.

Arugula Salad with Pomegranate Arils

Servings: 4 | Amount per serving: 90g or 3 oz. | Preparation Time: 10 minutes

INGREDIENTS:

- 4 cups arugula
- ½ cup cherry tomatoes, halved
- 4 Tbsp. of pomegranate arils
- 1 tsp. chives, fresh, chopped
- 1 tsp. tarragon, fresh, chopped
- 1 tsp. parsley, fresh, chopped
- Toasted walnuts (optional)

Dressing:
- 1 Tbsp. lemon juice
- ½ Tbsp. balsamic vinegar
- 1 Tbsp. extra-virgin olive oil
- Salt to tast

DIRECTIONS:

Toss salad ingredients together and dress with the vinaigrette.

Arugula Salad with Raw Pecans

Servings: 4 | Amount per serving: 90g or 3 oz.
Preparation Time: 10 minutes

INGREDIENTS:

- 1/2 cup pecans, baked
- 7 ounces arugula
- 2 apples, small, tart & sweet, peeled, thinly sliced
- 1/4 red onion, sliced
- 2 Tbsp. dried cranberries

Dressing:
- 1 lemon, juiced
- 3 Tbsp. olive oil
- 1-2 Dates
- Sea salt & black pepper to taste

NUTRITIONAL INFORMATION:

Energy (calories): 305kcal

Carbohydrates: 4.34 g

Protein: 2.92g

Fats: 32.03 g

Fiber: 1.5g

DIRECTIONS: Toss salad ingredients together and dress with the vinaigrette.

Chef Salad with Creamy Mayo Dressing

Servings: 4 | Amount per Serving: 280g or 12.3 oz.
Preparation Time: 10 minutes

INGREDIENTS:

- 8 cups mixed greens
- 4 green onions sliced
- 4 tomatoes sliced or wedged
- 2 cups cucumber, sliced

Dressing:
- 4 tbsp. Creamy Vegan Mayo Dressing
- Salt and pepper to taste

NUTRITIONAL INFORMATION:

Energy (calories): 99kcal

Carbohydrates: 10.94 g

Protein: 4.28 g

Fat: 5.24 g

Fiber 5.3g

DIRECTIONS:

Wash and dry the lettuce. Tear into bite size pieces and place in a large bowl. Top with remaining ingredients. Pour over the Creamy Vegan Mayo Dressing, toss and serve.

Fennel Orange Salad

Servings: 4 | Amount per Serving: 170g or 5.6 oz.
Preparation Time: 10 minutes

INGREDIENTS:

- 1 fennel bulb
- 1 large shallot
- 2 small oranges: blood orange or Cara Cara
- 2 Tbsp. pistachios, chopped
- 5 oz. baby mixed greens

For Citrus Salad Dressing:
- 1 Tbsp. orange juice, plus zest of 1/4 orange
- 1 Tbsp. lemon juice
- ¼ Tbsp. Dijon mustard
- Salt and pepper to taste
- 4 Tbsp. olive oil

NUTRITIONAL INFORMATION:

Energy (calories): 195kcal

Carbohydrates: 13.78 g

Protein: 2.89 g

Fat: 15.52 g

Fiber 4.8g

DIRECTIONS:

Make the Citrus Salad Dressing: mix all ingredients together. Thinly slice the fennel and the shallot. Cut oranges into sections. To serve, place the greens on a plate. Top with oranges, fennel, shallot, and chopped pistachios. Drizzle with dressing and serve.

Cucumber Dill Salad

Servings: 4 | Amount per Serving: 120g or 4 oz.
Preparation Time: 10 minutes

INGREDIENTS:

- 2 cucumbers, sliced
- 1 spring onion, sliced
- 1/4 cup white vinegar

- 2 Tbsp. oil
- 1-1/2 tsp. dried dill, or to taste
- Salt and pepper to taste

NUTRITIONAL INFORMATION:

Energy (calories): 78kcal

Carbohydrates: 2.81 g

Protein: 0.73g

Fats: 7.03 g

Fiber: 0.9g

DIRECTIONS:

Toss together the cucumbers and onion in a large bowl. Combine oil with vinegar, and salt. Drizzle over the salad and sprinkle with fresh dill. Serve.

Spinach Salad with Citrus and Roasted Beets

Servings: 4 | Amount per Serving: 290g or 10 oz.
Preparation Time: 10 minutes | Cooking Time: 1 hour 15 minutes

INGREDIENTS:

- 4 small beets, pre-roasted
- 1 Tbsp. extra-virgin olive oil
- ½ small red onion, sliced
- 1 tangerine, peeled, sectioned
- 1 large red grapefruit, peeled, sectioned
- 1 ½ Tbsp. Dijon mustard
- Salt and pepper to taste
- 1 Tbsp. red wine vinegar
- ¾ lbs. curly leaf spinach, stemmed, torn into bite-size pieces)

NUTRITIONAL INFORMATION:

Energy (calories): 130kcal

Carbohydrates: 21.62 g

Protein: 4.7g

Fats: 4.16 g

Fiber: 5.8g

DIRECTIONS:

Roast beets in oven at 400 until tender. Meanwhile, in a small bowl, mix all salad ingredients. Drizzle the mustard dressing over the salad and toss well. Serve right away.

---

7 Spice Mediterranean Tabbouleh Salad

Servings: 4 | Amount per serving: 90g or 3 oz.
Preparation Time: 10 minutes | Cooking Time: 1 hour 15 minutes

INGREDIENTS:

- ¾ cup pre-cooked barely
- ½ cup pomegranate seeds
- 1 cup red onion, minced
- 1 cup chickpeas, finely chopped (or 1/2 cup shelled hemp seeds and 1/2 cup chickpeas)
- 1 cup cucumber, chopped
- 1 cup red onion, minced
- 2 cups scallions, finely chopped
- 1-2 medium red tomatoes, finely chopped
- 1-2 medium yellow tomatoes, finely chopped
- ½ cup fresh black mint, chopped
- 2 cups parsley, finely chopped
- 1 tsp. allspice (optional)
- ¼ tsp. cumin, ground (optional)
- 1 tsp. black pepper, ground
- ½ cup lemon juice
- ½ cup olive oil
- Sea salt

NUTRITIONAL INFORMATION:

Energy (calories): 246kcal

Carbohydrates: 26.2g

Protein: 4.6 g

Fat: 13.93 g

Fiber 2.6g

DIRECTIONS:

Combine all the ingredients to a large mixing bowl. Mix well and stored in an airtight container in the fridge. Add lemon and olive oil dressing before serving.

Many Colors Joseph Salad

Servings: 4 - 6

INGREDIENTS:

- ½ of head romaine lettuce or mixes greens chopped
- 1-2 red roasted peppers, sliced into thin strips
- ½ green bell pepper, sliced into thin strips
- ½ yellow pepper, sliced into thin strips
- 1 cucumber, sliced thin
- 1 small red onion, sliced thin and separated into rings
- 2-3 medium red tomatoes, sliced
- 1 purple tomato, sliced
- ½ cup of mixed olives (black, green)
- 1 cup of mix of: lemon, orange slices, pomegranate and hemp seeds
- ½ cup (75 g) walnuts or almonds
- Pinch of cayenne pepper, sea salt, spices and olive oil to taste

DIRECTIONS:

Mix all salad ingredients in a bowl. Garnish with roasted red pepper sliced into thin strips, nuts, pomegranate seeds and spices. Enjoy!

Mixed Green Salad

Servings: 4 | Amount per Serving: 350 g or 3 oz.
Preparation Time: 10 minutes

INGREDIENTS:

- 1 head romaine lettuce
- 2 cucumber, peeled and sliced
- 3 plum tomatoes, cored and cut into small wedges
- 1 small red onion, sliced thin
- 3 Tbsp. olive oil
- 1 tsp. red wine vinegar, or more to taste
- Salt and pepper

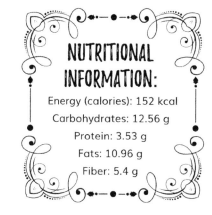

NUTRITIONAL INFORMATION:
Energy (calories): 152 kcal
Carbohydrates: 12.56 g
Protein: 3.53 g
Fats: 10.96 g
Fiber: 5.4 g

DIRECTIONS:

Tear the lettuce leaves into bite-sized pieces and transfer them to a large salad bowl. Add the cucumber, tomatoes, and onion. Sprinkle with the oil, vinegar, and salt and pepper, and toss to combine.

Avocado Salad

Servings: 4 | Amount per Serving: 120g or 4.2 oz.
Preparation Time: 10 minutes

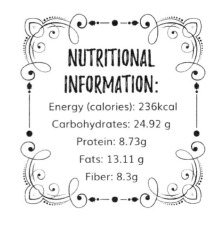

NUTRITIONAL INFORMATION:

Energy (calories): 236kcal

Carbohydrates: 24.92 g

Protein: 8.73g

Fats: 13.11 g

Fiber: 8.3g

INGREDIENTS:

- 6 cups organic kale, chopped, with the thick stems removed
- 4 Tbsp. sunflower seeds, raw, unsalted
- 2 Tbsp. almonds, pre-soaked, raw, sliced
- 1 cup purple cabbage, shredded
- ½ cup alfalfa sprouts
- 1 cup mix: chickpeas, black beans, lentils pre-soaked
- 4-6 Tbsp. sauerkraut
- 2 sheet of nori paper, sliced into smaller pieces

Dressing:
- 2 avocados, mashed
- 4 Tbsp. of lime juice,
- Salt and pepper to taste
- 1 tsp. of chili flakes
- 2 garlic clove, crushed

DIRECTIONS:

Massage dressing into the kale and let it sit for at least 5 minutes. Add other ingredients and toss.

Green Bean Salad with Cannellini Mayo Dressing

Servings: 4 | Amount per serving: : 440 g or 14.6 oz.
Preparation Time: 10 minutes

NUTRITIONAL INFORMATION:

Energy (calories): 476 kcal

Carbohydrates: 71.94 g

Protein: 28.03 g

Fats: 11.69 g

Fiber: 20.6 g

INGREDIENTS:

- 8 cups of green beans, stalks and ends trimmed
- 4 shallots, finely sliced
- 1 clove garlic, grated
- 4 tbsp. pine nuts
- 4 tbsp. pumpkin seeds
- ½ tsp. ground black pepper

DIRECTIONS:

Trim ends of beans and leave them whole. Drop beans into a saucepan with salted boiling water. Cook until crisp tender, about 3 to 5 minutes according to the size of the beans. Do not overcook. Drain and let cool. Combine the rest of ingredients and toss with Cannellini Mayo Dressing.

Mixed Green Salad with Avocado Dressing

Servings: 4 | Amount per Serving: 180g or 6 oz.

INGREDIENTS:

- 5 oz. spring lettuce mix
- 1 cup grape tomatoes, cut in half lengthwise
- 1 cup cucumber, sliced, seeded, peeled
- 1 cup sliced (1/8 inch) halved red onion

Dressing:
- 1 avocado, mashed
- 4 Tbsp. of olive oil
- 3 Tbsp. unsweetened, almond milk
- 2 tsp. onion powder
- 1½ tsp. white wine vinegar
- 1½ tsp. garlic powder
- Sea salt and pepper, to taste
- 2 tsp. fresh parsley, chopped
- 2 tsp. fresh dill, chopped
2 tsp. fresh chives, chopped

NUTRITIONAL INFORMATION:

Energy (calories): 243kcal

Carbohydrates: 13.79 g

Protein: 2.73g

Fiber: 5.3g

DIRECTIONS:

In large salad bowl, place salad ingredients. Pour dressing over salad; toss gently to mix.

Quinoa Nut Pilaf Salad

Servings: 4 | Amount per serving: 330g or 11 oz.
Preparation Time: 10 minutes | Cooking Time: 25 minutes

INGREDIENTS:

- 3 tbsp. extra virgin olive oil, divided (2 tbsp. and 1 tbsp.)
- 1 onion, finely chopped
- 1 bell pepper, finely chopped
- 1 garlic clove, minced
- 2 tbsp. pine nuts
- 1 ½ cup (255g) uncooked quinoa
- 3 cups water to cook quinoa
- Pinch freshly ground black pepper
- 2 tbsp. fresh mint, chopped
- 2 tbsp. fresh basil, chopped
- 1 tbsp. fresh chives or scallions, chopped
- 1 small cucumber, peeled, seeds removed, chopped
- 1 tsp. of salt
- ¼ tsp. of black pepper

DIRECTIONS:

Boil quinoa until cooked, strain and let cool. Chop all veggies and mix with cooked quinoa. Add oil and spices. Mix. Serve chilled or at room temperature.

Lemon-Parsley Bean Salad

Servings: 4 | Amount per Serving: 320 g or 10.6 oz.
Preparation Time: 5 minutes | Cooking Time: 20 minutes

NUTRITIONAL INFORMATION:

Energy (calories): 425 kcal

Carbohydrates: 54.69 g

Protein: 18.62 g

Fats: 16.56 g

Fiber: 16.6 g

INGREDIENTS:

- 3 cups kidney beans, cooked
- 1 ½ cups chickpeas, cooked
- 1 small red onion, diced
- 2 stalks celery, sliced in half or thirds lengthwise and chopped
- 1 medium cucumber, peeled, seeded and diced

Dressing:
- ¾ cup fresh parsley, chopped
- 2 tbsp. fresh dill or mint, chopped
- ¼ cup olive oil
- ¼ cup fresh lemon juice
- 3 cloves garlic, pressed or minced
- ¾ tsp. salt
- Small pinch red pepper flakes

DIRECTIONS:

In a serving bowl, combine the prepared kidney beans, chickpeas, onion, celery, cucumber, parsley and dill (or mint). Make the lemon dressing: In a small bowl, whisk together the olive oil, lemon juice, garlic, salt and pepper flakes until emulsified. Pour dressing over the bean and vegetable mixture and toss thoroughly. Serve.

Mexican Salad

Servings: 4 | Amount per Serving: 390 g or 13 oz.
Preparation Time: 5 minutes | Cooking Time: 15 minutes

NUTRITIONAL INFORMATION:

Energy (calories): 370 kcal

Carbohydrates: 35.02 g

Protein: 8.76 g

Fats: 24.86 g

Fiber: 14 g

INGREDIENTS:

- 2 tsp. olive oil
- 1 ear corn husks and silk removed
- 2 bell peppers red and green
- 4 medium-sized tomatoes red and yellow
- ½ red of onion
- 2 scallions
- 1 avocado, pitted
- 170 grams or 1 cup black beans pre-boiled or canned

For Avocado Dressing:
Use recipe in the Dips, Dressings and Sauces section.

DIRECTIONS:

Use a broiler or a griddle pan to grill corn. Heat a lug of olive oil over medium-high heat and grill the whole corn cob for 15 minutes, lid closed, turning every 5 minutes, until the cob has black burn marks here and there and the kernels are soft (you can check it by piercing the cob with a fork). Let it cool a bit and remove the kernels with a knife. While your corn is grilling, chop the veggies. Dice red and green bell pepper, red and yellow tomatoes, red onion, scallions and avocado and arrange in four bowls or plates, creating sections (or just toss it all together if you prefer). Add already boiled (or canned and rinsed) black beans and the broiled corn kernels. Pour the dressing over the salad. Enjoy!

Eggplant Salad with Roasted Tomatoes

Servings: 4 | Amount per Serving: 550 g or 18.3 oz.
Preparation Time: 15 minutes | Cooking Time: 35 minutes

INGREDIENTS:

- 2 cups (220g) cherry tomatoes, sliced in half
- 3 small eggplants
- 1 ½ cups (255g) uncooked quinoa
- 1 cup (160g) cooked chickpeas, cooked
- 1 garlic clove, minced
- ½ cup (70g) pine nuts, toasted
- 3 cups arugula
- 3 Tbsp. basil
- 1 Tbsp. olive oil (optional)
- Sea salt & freshly ground black pepper

NUTRITIONAL INFORMATION:
Energy (calories): 545 kcal
Carbohydrates: 78.72 g
Protein: 19.4 g
Fats: 20.75 g
Fiber: 22.3 g

DIRECTIONS:

Cook quinoa, set aside. Chop the eggplant into 1 inch pieces and place on a paper towel with a few pinches of salt. Let it sit for about 20 minutes. As water releases from the eggplant flesh, pat it dry. Preheat the oven to 300°F and line a baking sheet with oiled parchment paper. Place the cherry tomatoes, eggplant, chickpea mixture, garlic, onion on the baking sheet and toss with a drizzle of olive oil and a few pinches of salt and pepper. Roast the veggies about 30-35 minutes. Add the roasted veggies, pine nuts, arugula and basil to a large bowl with the cooked quinoa. Drizzle it with olive oil (optional) and season with salt and pepper. Optional - add sherry vinegar, to taste. Serve and enjoy.

Roasted Brussels Sprouts with Cranberries

Servings: 4 | Amount per Serving: 290 g or 9.6 oz.
Preparation Time: 5 minutes | Cooking Time: 15 minutes

INGREDIENTS:

- 36 oz. of Brussels sprouts, trimmed & halved
- 6 Tbsp. olive oil
- A pinch salt
- 8 Tbsp. (60g) cranberries, dried

DIRECTIONS:

Toss the Brussels Sprouts with olive oil. Season the sprouts with a bit of salt before roasting, water sauté them in a skillet, over medium high heat for 15 minutes, then cover them, and let them steam for next 5 minutes; they will have started to soften. Remove the sprouts from the skillet and scatter over the cranberries. Serve.

Portobello Chickpea Salad

Servings: 4 | Amount per serving: 420 g or 14 oz.
Preparation Time: 10 minutes | Cooking Time: 15 minutes

NUTRITIONAL INFORMATION:

Energy (calories): 717 kcal
Carbohydrates: 46.74 g
Protein: 16.96 g
Fats: 54.96 g
Fiber: 15.8 g

INGREDIENTS:

- 4 Portobello mushrooms (~11 oz.), stems removed.
- 1/3 cup olive oil
- 2 1/2 tbsp. tamari (soy)sauce
- 2 tbsp. balsamic vinegar
- 1 shallot, finely chopped
- 1 clove garlic, minced or crushed
- 1/2 tsp. hot smoked paprika
- 1 tsp. dried oregano
- 1/2 tsp. dried thyme

Dressing:
- 1/4 cup mustard
- 1/4 cup red wine vinegar
- 4 tbsp. olive oil

Salad:
- 3/4 cup mixed raw nuts (such as cashews, pecans, walnuts, almonds), chopped
- 2 cups chickpeas, cooked
- 6 cups mixed salad greens
- 2 shallots or 1 small red onion, sliced into half moons
- 1 avocado, sliced into half moons
- 1/2 cup cherry tomatoes, halved

DIRECTIONS:

Start by preparing the mushrooms. In a small bowl, whisk together the olive oil, tamari, balsamic vinegar, shallots, garlic, paprika, oregano and thyme. Pour a small portion of the mixture into a large shallow glass baking dish. Place the mushrooms top-side down and pour the rest of the mixture over the mushrooms. Coat the mushrooms thoroughly with a pastry brush and let sit for 30 minutes to marinate. Meanwhile, in a small unoiled saucepan, toast the nuts over medium heat, stirring or tossing often, until lightly browned. Set aside. In a small bowl, whisk together all of the ingredients for the dressing, and set aside. In a large salad bowl, toss the chickpeas, mixed greens, and shallots or red onion with the dressing. To cook the mushrooms, preheat an oven to 400°F. Bake the mushrooms for 15 minutes, flip, and bake for another 10 minutes. Take care not to overcook the mushrooms — they should be succulent in texture. Remove from heat and let rest for a few minutes before slicing. To serve, place the dressed salad onto serving plates. Top with slices of mushroom and garnish with toasted nuts, slices of avocado, and cherry tomatoes.

Raw Sunflower Tuna Salad

Servings: 2 | Preparation Time: 10 minutes

INGREDIENTS:

- 1 ½ cups raw sunflower seeds, soaked
- 2 stalks celery, diced
- 1 tbsp. dulse flakes
- 2 tbsp. dill, fresh
- 2 scallions (diced)

DIRECTIONS:

Grind the sunflower seeds in the food processor to tuna texture. In a large mixing bowl toss all ingredients and mix thoroughly. Serve with vegan mayonnaise on romaine lettuce wraps or on top of a salad. Enjoy!

Lentil Kale Salad

Servings: 4 | Amount per Serving: : 250g or 8.3 oz.
Preparation Time: 10 minutes | Cooking Time: 15 minutes

INGREDIENTS:

- 10 oz. large bunch Tuscan kale
- Kosher salt
- ½ cup raw almonds
- 3 scallions
- 4 garlic cloves
- 1 lemon
- ½ cup extra-virgin olive oil
- 1½ cups black beluga or French green lentils
- 1 Tbsp. cumin seeds
- ½ tsp. crushed red pepper flakes
- 1 cup Castelvetrano olives

NUTRITIONAL INFORMATION:

Energy (calories): 662kcal
Carbohydrates: 60.67 g
Protein: 24.72g
Fats: 39.16 g
Fibers: 13.7g

DIRECTIONS:

Strip leaves off stems from 1 large bunch Tuscan kale; discard stems. Stack leaves, and then roll into fat cigars. Slice crosswise into ¼" strips to make long, thin ribbons. Unfurl ribbons and run your knife through them just once or twice more to shorten any very long strips. Transfer to a large bowl, season with salt, and massage until kale is silkier, softer, and darker in color, 1–2 minutes. Bring a large pot of heavily salted water to a boil over high heat. Prepare the spiced oil. Coarsely chop ½ cup raw almonds; set aside. Trim 3 scallions and separate white and green parts (save the green parts for later in the recipe); thinly slice white parts and transfer to a small skillet. Peel and crush 4 garlic cloves. Add those to same skillet, too. Using a vegetable peeler or paring knife, remove three 3" strips of lemon peel (avoiding white pith); reserve rest of the lemon for your salad dressing. Add peels to skillet. Pour ½ cup extra-virgin olive oil into skillet and stir so that all of the elements are coated in oil. Add 1½ cups black beluga or French green lentils to now-boiling water, reduce heat to medium, and simmer, uncovered, until lentils are tender but still al dente, 20–25 minutes.

While lentils cook, heat skillet with scallion mixture over medium. Cook, stirring occasionally, until garlic starts to brown and lemon peel starts to curl, about 3 minutes. Add almonds and cook, stirring frequently, until almonds are browned, about 3 more minutes. Remove from heat and stir in 1 Tbsp. cumin seeds and ½ tsp. crushed red pepper flakes. Strain mixture through a fine-mesh sieve into a small bowl, shaking to help oil drain; reserve oil (that's the base of your salad dressing). Spread almond mixture (with cumin seeds) on a paper towel-lined plate or baking sheet. Season with salt and let cool (the nuts will get crunchier as they sit).Smash 1 cup Castelvetrano olives with the back of your knife; remove pits. Tear olives into large pieces and add to bowl. Thinly slice reserved scallion greens and add most to bowl (save some for serving). Add juice of reserved lemon and ½ tsp. salt. Drain lentils well, and add to bowl with kale; season with salt. Add infused oil and half of nuts and toss to combine. Divide salad among bowls. Garnish with remaining nuts and scallion greens.

Roasted Vegetable Salad with Lime Green Sauce

Servings: 4 | Amount per Serving: : 500 g or 1.1 lbs.
Preparation Time: 15 minutes | Cooking Time: 30 minutes

INGREDIENTS:

- 2 large sweet potatoes, halved
- 4 whole carrots, halved and chopped
- 2 Tbsp. of olive oil, divided
- 2 tsp. curry powder, divided
- 1 tsp. sea salt, divided
- 2 cup broccoli, chopped
- 4 cups red cabbage, chopped
- 2 red bell peppers, medium

Magic Green Sauce
- 10 cloves garlic, peeled and crushed
- 2 medium Serrano or jalapeño pepper
- 2 cup packed cilantro, stems cut off
- 2 cup packed flat-leaf parsley
- ½ ripe avocado
- ½ tsp. salt, plus more to taste
- 6 Tbsp. lime juice
- Water to thin ~3 Tbsp.

Salad
- 8 cups hearty greens (spinach, kale, or mustard greens), chopped
- 1 medium ripe avocado, chopped
- 6 Tbsp. hemp seeds
- 1 Tbsp. of fresh herbs (cilantro, parsley, thyme, etc.)
- 10-14 medium sliced radishes

NUTRITIONAL INFORMATION:

Energy (calories):438 kcal

Carbohydrates: 48.91 g

Protein: 11.74 g

Fats: 25.91 g

Fiber: 16.8 g

DIRECTIONS:

Preheat oven to 375 °F (190 C) and line 2 baking sheets with parchment paper. Add the sweet potato and carrots to one baking sheet and toss with half of the oil, half of the curry powder, and half of the sea salt. Bake for 25 minutes total or until golden brown and tender. To a separate baking sheet, add broccoli, cabbage, and bell pepper and toss with remaining half of the oil, half of the curry powder, and half of the sea salt. Bake for 15-20 minutes total or until golden brown and tender (place in oven once the potatoes have been cooking for 5-10 minutes. In the meantime, make magic green sauce. Place garlic and pepper in a food processor along with the cilantro, parsley, avocado, salt and lime juice. Process/mix until smooth, scraping down sides as needed. Thin with water until a semi-thick (but pourable) sauce is formed. Plate salad by adding mixed greens to a serving platter and topping with roasted vegetables. Arrange avocado along the edges, along with radishes. Sprinkle the top with hemp seeds and serve with dressing on the side. Garnish with herbs if desired.

Asian Salad with Sesame Ginger Dressing

Servings: 4 | Amount per Serving: 180g or 6 oz.
Preparation Time: 10 minutes

INGREDIENTS:

- 4 carrots, grated
- 1 large red pepper, finely diced
- 2 celery stalks, finely diced
- ½ medium red onion, finely diced
- ½ cup cilantro or parsley, chopped
- 4 Tbsp. toasted sesame seeds
- ½ cup roasted peanuts, almonds, or cashews

Dressing:
- 3 Tbsp. of sesame oil
- 2 Tbsp. fresh squeezed lemon juice
- 2 tsp. soy sauce
- 1 Tbsp. of grated ginger
- 1 small clove of garlic, crushed
- Sea salt to taste

NUTRITIONAL INFORMATION:

Energy (calories): 286kcal

Carbohydrates: 17.06 g

Protein: 7.76g

Fats: 23.9 g

Fibers: 6.2g

DIRECTIONS:

Combine all the dressing ingredients in a small bowl and whisk together. Set aside. Toss all the remaining ingredients together in a medium-sized bowl. Pour over the dressing and toss to coat.

Cranberry Cilantro Quinoa Salad

Servings: 4 | Amount per Serving: 550g or 19.4 oz.
Preparation Time: 15 minutes

INGREDIENTS:

- 1 ½ cup quinoa, precooked
- 4 Tbsp. of dried cranberries
- 2 cups of cucumber, chopped
- 9 Tbsp. fresh cilantro, chopped
- 2 cups of bell pepper, diced
- 4 roasted peppers, diced
- 4 tomatoes, chopped
- 4 Tbsp. almonds, toasted, sliced
- 8 Tbsp. carrots, grated/shredded
- 1 lime, juice
- 1 lemon, juice
- 1 cup green chopped onion
- Salt and pepper to taste
- Olive oil for drizzling as desired
- Pinch of cumin or to taste (optional)
- 1 additional lime sliced into wedges to garnish

NUTRITIONAL INFORMATION:

Energy (calories): 527kcal

Carbohydrates: 88.66 g

Protein: 18.72g

Fats: 13.38 g

Fibers: 14.5g

DIRECTIONS:

Combine freshly cooked quinoa with all the vegetables and nuts. Season to taste. For best results, chill salad before serving. Enjoy!

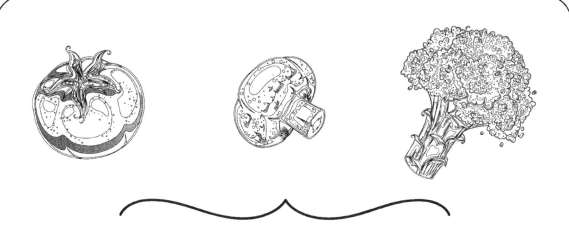

"Behold, I stand at the door and knock. If anyone hears my voice and opens the door, I will come in to him and eat with him, and he with me."

Revelation 3:20

Soup Recipes

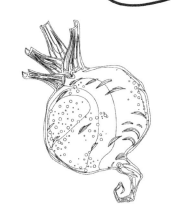

Spiced Carrot Lentil Soup

Servings: 4 | Amount per Serving: 560 g or 19.7 oz.
Preparation Time: 10 minutes | Cooking Time: 20 minutes

INGREDIENTS:

- 2 Tbsp. cumin seeds
- Pinch chili flakes
- 4 Tbsp. olive oil
- 20 oz. carrots washed, coarsely grated
- 7 oz. split red lentils
- 6 cups homemade vegetable broth
- 4 Tbsp. flaxseeds, ground

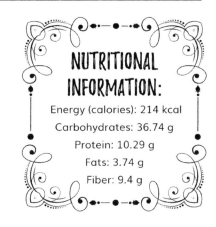

NUTRITIONAL INFORMATION:

Energy (calories): 403 kcal

Carbohydrates: 47.24 g

Protein: 13.57 g

Fats: 19.5 g

Fiber: 12 g

DIRECTIONS:

Heat a large saucepan and dry roast cumin seeds and a pinch of chili flakes for 1 min, or until they start to jump around the pan and release their aromas. Scoop out about half with a spoon and set aside. Add olive oil, carrots, red lentils, and hot vegetable stock and bring to boil. Cook for 20 mins until the lentils have swollen and softened. Season to taste and add ground flaxseeds. Finish with sprinkling of the reserved toasted spices.

Minestrone Soup

Servings: 4 | Amount per Serving: 400 g or 13.3 oz.
Preparation Time: 10 minutes | Cooking Time: 25 minutes

INGREDIENTS:

- 1 onion, chopped
- 2 stalks celery, chopped
- 2 carrots, chopped
- 2 cloves garlic, chopped
- 1 medium zucchini, diced
- ¼ tsp. sea salt
- 1 potato, diced
- 1/8 tsp. black pepper
- 7 oz. kidney beans, cooked
- 7 oz. garbanzo beans, cooked
- 16 oz. vegetable broth
- 1 Tbsp. Italian spice
- 12 oz. tomato juice

NUTRITIONAL INFORMATION:

Energy (calories): 214 kcal

Carbohydrates: 36.74 g

Protein: 10.29 g

Fats: 3.74 g

Fiber: 9.4 g

DIRECTIONS:

Clean and chop vegetables. In a large pot, add veggie broth, tomato juice, onion, celery, salt, pepper, Italian spices. Let boil for 5 minutes. Add carrots and potato. Boil until carrots are al dente. Add zucchini, beans, garlic and boil until zucchini is soft but not mushy. Taste and adjust seasonings, if necessary.

Red Lentil Tomato Kale Soup

Servings: 4 | Amount per serving: : 520 g or 18.3 oz.
Preparation Time: 10 minutes | Cooking Time: 35 minutes

INGREDIENTS:

- 14 oz. canned tomatoes, diced
- 5-6 cups vegetable broth
- 1 cup red lentils (190g), rinsed and drained
- 2 cups (60g) spinach or kale or mix
- Salt and pepper, to taste
- 1 Tbsp. coconut oil
- 2 large garlic cloves, minced
- 1 onion, diced
- 3 celery stalks, diced
- 1 Tsp. cumin, ground
- 2 Tsp. chili powder

NUTRITIONAL INFORMATION:

Energy (calories): 258kcal
Carbohydrates: 42.91 g
Protein: 13.36g
Fats: 5.13 g
Fiber: 8.6g

DIRECTIONS:

In a large pot, water sauté the onion and garlic for about 5-6 minutes over medium heat. Add in the celery and sauté for a few minutes more. Stir in the spices (cumin, chili powder). Stir in the can of tomatoes including juice, broth, and lentils. Bring to a boil, reduce heat, and then simmer, uncovered, for about 20-25 minutes, until lentils are tender and fluffy. Stir in spinach and season to taste adding more spices if you wish.

Italian Bean and Kale Soup

Servings: 4 | Amount per serving: 160g or 5.3 oz.
Preparation Time: 15 minutes | Cooking Time: 20 minutes

INGREDIENTS:

- 2 cups kale, chopped
- 2 medium sized potatoes, diced
- 1- 15 oz. can white beans, drained
- 1 small onion, diced
- 1 clove garlic, minced
- ½ tsp. garlic powder
- 1 tsp. fresh rosemary, chopped
- 1-3 Tbsp. powdered vegetable bouillon (optional)
- ½ cup plant nut milk
- 32 oz. vegetable stock

NUTRITIONAL INFORMATION:

Energy (calories): 319kcal
Carbohydrates: 61.4 g
Protein: 13.34 g
Fats: 2.94 g
Fiber: 9.3 g

DIRECTIONS:

Water sauté onion. Add garlic, vegetable stock, potatoes, and bring to a boil. Boil until potatoes are tender then add the rest of the ingredients except kale and rosemary, turn off heat. Blend a portion of the soup and add back to the pot. Turn heat on low and add the kale and rosemary. Cook for 5 minutes, turn off heat. Serve and enjoy!

Mushroom Barley Soup

Servings: 4 | Amount per Serving: 320 g or 10.6 oz.
Preparation Time: 10 minutes | Cooking Time: 20 minutes

INGREDIENTS:

- 3 Tbsp. vegan butter
- 1 medium onion, chopped
- 1 cup carrots, diced
- 1/2 cup celery, chopped
- 1 clove garlic, chopped
- 11 oz. fresh mushrooms, sliced
- 3¼ cups vegetable broth
- ½ cup barley
- ½ Tbsp. Bragg organic sprinkle seasoning
- 1 Tbsp. Italian spice
- Salt and pepper to taste

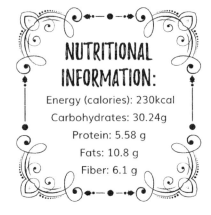

NUTRITIONAL INFORMATION:

Energy (calories): 230kcal

Carbohydrates: 30.24g

Protein: 5.58 g

Fats: 10.8 g

Fiber: 6.1 g

DIRECTIONS:

In a large pot, add vegetable broth, barley and salt to boil. Cook until barley is al dente. Add all vegetables and spices. Simmer until vegetables are soft but not mushy. Season with salt and pepper before serving.

Tomato Barley Vegetable Soup

Servings: 4 | Amount per Serving: 450 g or 1 lb.
Preparation Time: 10 minutes | Cooking Time: 45 minutes

INGREDIENTS:

- 3 Tbsp. olive oil
- 2 ribs celery, chopped
- 2 medium carrots, chopped
- ½ onions, chopped
- 2 to 3 cloves garlic, minced
- 3 cups vegetable broth
- Dash pepper or to taste
- 16 oz. can diced tomatoes, do not drain
- 1 cup barley grains
- ½ tsp. Italian seasoning
- 2 cups fresh spinach
- Dash salt or to taste

NUTRITIONAL INFORMATION:

Energy (calories): 464kcal

Carbohydrates: 55.84g

Protein: 8.56 g

Fats: 25.53 g

Fiber: 9.2 g

DIRECTIONS:

In a large soup or stock pan, heat onions and garlic for a minute or two, then add the chopped carrots and celery. Heat for 4 to 5 minutes, just to start the vegetables cooking a bit with a head start. Add the can of diced tomatoes (do not drain), the vegetable broth, barley, and the Italian seasoning, stirring well to combine. Bring to a boil, cover, and then reduce to a medium-low simmer. Cook for 30 to 40 minutes or until barley is cooked. You may need to add a little bit of extra water or vegetable broth. Once the barley is cooked, stir in the fresh spinach and heat for one more minute (just until spinach wilted), then turn off heat. Season your soup generously with salt and pepper.

Indian Lentil Collard Soup

Servings: 4 | Amount per serving: : 550 g or 18.3 oz.
Preparation Time: 10 minutes | Cooking Time: 35 minutes

INGREDIENTS:

- ¼ cup extra virgin olive oil
- 1 medium yellow or white onion, chopped
- 2 carrots, peeled and chopped
- 4 garlic cloves, pressed or minced
- 2 tsp. ground cumin
- 1 tsp. curry powder
- ½ tsp. dried thyme
- 1 large can (28 oz.) diced tomatoes, lightly drained
- 1 cup brown or green lentils, rinsed
- 4 cups vegetable broth
- 2 cups water
- 1 tsp. salt, more to taste
- Pinch of red pepper flakes
- Freshly ground black pepper to taste
- 1 cup collard greens, chopped
- 1 tsp. garam masala
- 1 lemon, juiced

NUTRITIONAL INFORMATION:

Energy (calories): 350kcal

Carbohydrates: 44.15g

Protein: 13.75 g

Fats: 14.74 g

Fiber: 8 g

DIRECTIONS:

Add all ingredients except collard greens and lemon to a large pot and bring to a boil. Simmer for 15- 20 minutes until veggies are cooked. Add collard greens and cook 1 more minute until wilted. Squeeze lemon into soup. Taste and adjust seasonings. Serve while hot.

Potato Corn Chowder

Servings: 4 | Amount per serving: 390g or 13 oz.
Preparation Time: 5 minutes | Cooking Time: 15 minutes

INGREDIENTS:

- 3 Tbsp. olive oil
- 1 medium carrots, peeled and chopped
- 1 stalk celery, chopped
- 1 yellow onion, chopped
- 2 cloves garlic, minced
- 2 Tbsp. oat flour
- ½ tsp. dried thyme leaves
- 1 ½ lbs. white or Yukon gold potatoes, peeled and diced
- 1 cup vegetable broth
- 1 cup of almond milk
- ½ cup fresh or frozen corn kernels
- ½ tsp. salt to taste
- 1/8 tsp. pepper to taste

NUTRITIONAL INFORMATION:

Energy (calories): 327kcal

Carbohydrates: 45.26 g

Protein: 5.04g

Fats: 14.57 g

Fiber: 6.2g

DIRECTIONS:

Directions: Heat the oil in a large soup pot over medium-high heat. When hot add the carrots, celery, onion and garlic. Water sauté until the vegetables just start to soften and the onion turns translucent and begins to brown, about 5 minutes. Sprinkle the oat flour and thyme over the vegetables and stir to coat. Continue to stir and cook for about a minute until the flour starts to brown. Stir in the potatoes, vegetable broth, and almond milk. Bring to a simmer and cook until the potatoes are fork tender and the chowder has thickened, about 8 minutes. Lastly, add in the corn and season with salt and pepper. If your chowder gets too thick, you can always thin it with water or a vegetable broth to the desired consistency. Serve hot.

Pumpkin Soup

Servings: 4 | Amount per Serving: 400 g or 13.3 oz.
Preparation Time: 10 minutes | Cooking Time: 25 minutes

INGREDIENTS:

- 3 Tbsp. oil
- 1 onion, diced
- 16 oz. pumpkin
- 1 1/3 cups of vegetable broth
- 3 cups almond milk
- ½ tsp. nutmeg
- 2 Tbsp. flaxseeds, ground
- Salt and pepper to taste

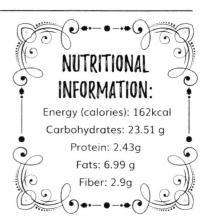

NUTRITIONAL INFORMATION:

Energy (calories): 225kcal

Carbohydrates: 20.39g

Protein: 4.52 g

Fats: 14.62 g

Fiber: 2.3 g

DIRECTIONS:

In a large saucepan, water sauté onion for 3-5 minutes, until onion turns clear. Add remaining ingredients, stirring to combine. Cook over medium heat for 10-15 minutes. Serve.

Spinach Potato Soup

Servings: 4 | Amount per Serving: 350g or 11.6 oz.
Preparation Time: 10 minutes | Cooking Time: 20 minutes

INGREDIENTS:

- 2 Tbsp. of oil
- 1 onion, chopped
- 1 leek, sliced
- 2 small sticks celery, sliced
- 1 small potato, peeled and diced
- ½ tsp. ground black pepper
- 1 quart of veggie stock
- 1 lb. spinach

NUTRITIONAL INFORMATION:

Energy (calories): 162kcal

Carbohydrates: 23.51 g

Protein: 2.43g

Fats: 6.99 g

Fiber: 2.9g

DIRECTIONS:

In a large pot, bring veggie stock and vegetables except spinach to boil. Cook for 10-15 minutes until potato is tender. Add spinach and cook for a few minutes more until wilted. You can eat as is or blend for creamy consistency.

Roasted Cauliflower Rosemary

Servings: 4 | Amount per Serving: 320g or 10.6oz.
Preparation Time: 5 minutes | Cooking Time: 15 minutes

INGREDIENTS:

- 3 Tbsp. olive oil
- 1 onion, chopped
- 1 clove garlic, crushed
- 1 tsp. dried thyme
- 1/2 tsp. dried rosemary
- 1 large head cauliflower, chopped
- 2 cups (480ml) vegetable stock
- 1 14oz. (400ml) almond milk
- Salt and pepper to taste
- To garnish; ½ cup roasted chickpeas, pinch nutmeg

NUTRITIONAL INFORMATION:

Energy (calories): 172kcal

Carbohydrates: 13.39 g

Protein: 3.3g

Fats: 12.36 g

Fiber: 2g

DIRECTIONS:

Mix the cauliflower, garlic, onion and spices and place them on a pan lined with oiled parchment paper. Bake in the oven at 375°F for 20 minutes until soft. Place in blender with a little vegetable stock and blend until smooth. Add this mix into the vegetable stock and almond milk and bring to boil and simmer for 5 minutes. Add salt and pepper if needed. Garnish with roasted chickpeas and nutmeg. Serve.

Cauliflower Leek Soup

Servings: 4 | Amount per Serving: 390 g
Preparation Time: 5 minutes | Cooking Time: 20 minutes

INGREDIENTS:

- 2 Tbsp. olive oil
- 1 leek, chopped
- 1 lemon, juiced
- 1 ½ lbs. cauliflower, cut into bite size
- 3 cups vegetable broth
- 3 Tbsp. flaxseeds, ground
- Salt and pepper to taste

NUTRITIONAL INFORMATION:

Energy (calories): 169kcal

Carbohydrates: 16.93 g

Protein: 5.06g

Fats: 10.58 g

Fiber: 6g

DIRECTIONS:

Put vegetable broth to boil in a pot. Add 1/4 tsp. of salt and the juice of 1 lemon. Add cauliflower and cook, uncovered, for 5 minutes. In meantime, water sauté chopped leek until it tenders, 10 minutes. Add chopped leeks to cauliflower broth and bring to boil. Cook for 3 minutes, remove from heat, add flax and blend with a handy mixer. Puree until smooth and serve.

Cabbage Detox Soup

Servings: 4
Amount per Serving: 730g–488g or 25.7 oz. to 17.2oz
Preparation Time: 10 minutes | Cooking Time: 20 minutes

INGREDIENTS:

- 6 cups veggie broth
- 2 onions, sliced or chopped
- 4 cloves garlic, minced
- 2 carrots, medium, peeled, diced
- 1 green, yellow, red, bell pepper, diced
- 1 cup celery, diced
- 1/2 head cabbage, chopped
- 1 tsp. lemon juice
- 1 tsp. organic apple cider vinegar
- 1 cup V8 vegetable juice
- 2-3 medium fresh tomatoes, diced
- 6 large fresh scallions, chopped
- ¼ tsp. black pepper
- 1 cup fresh spinach or bok choy
- 1 tsp. oregano
- 1 tsp. basil
- ¼ tsp. salt
- 2 bay leaves
- ¼ tsp. fresh parsley or cilantro, chopped
- 2 tbsp. sunflower or grape seed oil
- Pinch of cayenne pepper (optional)

NUTRITIONAL INFORMATION:

Energy (calories): 234 kcal

Carbohydrates: 41.2 g

Protein: 8.34 g

Fats: 5.88 g

Fiber: 7.4 g

DIRECTIONS:

Bring veggie broth to a boil in a pot. Add all the ingredients except the scallions and spinach. Reduce heat to simmer. Cook until vegetables are tender, about 15 minutes. Add the spinach and cook for 3-5 min. Taste broth and adjust seasoning if needed. Garnish with ¼ tsp. fresh parsley or cilantro. Serve and enjoy!

Green Power Soup

Servings: 8 | Amount per Serving: 380 g 13.4oz
Preparation Time: 30 minutes | Cooking Time: 10 minutes

INGREDIENTS:

- 1 onion, rough chopped
- 3 cloves garlic, rough chopped
- ½" ginger, rough chopped
- 8 cups vegetable stock
- 1 cup cauliflower
- 1 cup broccoli
- 2 small leeks
- ½ bunch kale ~4 cups, chopped
- 4 cups spinach, fresh or frozen
- Juice of half a lemon

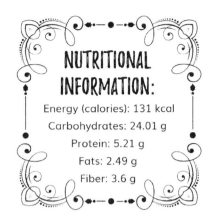

NUTRITIONAL INFORMATION:
Energy (calories): 131 kcal
Carbohydrates: 24.01 g
Protein: 5.21 g
Fats: 2.49 g
Fiber: 3.6 g

DIRECTIONS:

Directions: Add vegetable broth and all ingredients except spinach and kale. Bring these to a boil and then turn it down to simmer for 10 minutes.

The vegetables should be tender when done. Now, add the kale and spinach and allow to simmer for another 4 minutes or until these are soft. Serve.

Potato Leek Soup with Roasted Chickpea

Servings: 6
Preparation Time: 15 minutes | Cooking Time: 1 hour

INGREDIENTS:

- 2 large leeks, thinly sliced
- 4-6 medium potatoes, peeled and diced
- 1/2 tsp. smoked paprika
- 3 cups vegetable broth
- 1 cup nut milk
- 1 stalk celery, diced
- 1 medium onion, diced
- 2 Tbsp. vegan butter
- 2 tsp. Italian seasoning
- Salt & freshly ground pepper

To garnish: 1 cup Roasted Chickpea, ¼ tsp. fresh parsley or cilantro.

NUTRITIONAL INFORMATION:
Energy (calories): 234 kcal
Carbohydrates: 41.2 g
Protein: 8.34 g
Fats: 5.88 g
Fiber: 7.4 g

DIRECTIONS:

In a large pot, add enough vegetable broth to just cover the vegetables and bring to a boil. Simmer until potatoes are done. Meanwhile, preheat the oven to 400 degrees F. Taste and adjust seasoning as needed. Garnish with ¼ tsp. fresh parsley or cilantro and roasted chickpea. Serve and enjoy!

Chef Notes: you can add 1 large sweet potato with coconut for Caribbean taste or Cajun spice mix (optional).

Make the roasted chickpeas: Melt 1 Tbsp. vegan butter or oil then mix with the paprika and spices and chickpeas in a bowl. Spread on a baking sheet and bake until golden, 8 to 10 minutes. When the roasted chickpea are ready, set aside.

Joana's Sancocho Soup

Servings: 6
Preparation Time: 15 minutes | Cooking Time: 1 hour

INGREDIENTS:

- 4 potatoes, cut in quarters
- 4 yuca, frozen
- 2 corn on the cob, cut in half
- 1 green large plantain, unripe, brake into thumb size pieces
- 4 cups vegetable broth
- 2 tsp. of Sazon spice mix
- 2 tsp. Adobo spice mix
- ½ tsp. cumin powder
- ¼ cup olive oil

NUTRITIONAL INFORMATION:
Energy (calories): 327kcal
Carbohydrates: 45.26 g
Protein: 5.04g
Fats: 14.57 g
Fiber: 6.2g

DIRECTIONS:

In a large pot, add enough vegetable broth to just cover the vegetables and bring to a boil. Cook until the vegetables are soft but not overcooked. Add all the spice mixes. Taste and adjust seasoning if needed. Season with salt and pepper. Serve in bowls garnished with the cilantro. Enjoy!

Bulgarian White Bean Soup "Bob Chorba"

Servings: 4
Preparation Time: 10 minutes | Cooking Time: 30 minutes

INGREDIENTS:

- 1 ½ lbs. dry white beans, soaked in water overnight, drained
- 2 large yellow onions, chopped
- 4 tbsp. sweet paprika
- Freshly ground pepper to taste
- 1 can (14.5 oz.) peeled tomatoes in tomato juice
- 6 tbsp. minced, fresh summer savory or 2 tsp. dried savory
- 4-5 tbsp. vegetable oil
- 2 small carrots, peeled, chopped
- 4 cloves garlic, peeled, chopped
- 2 stalks celery, chopped
- Salt to taste
- 8 cups water + extra to cook the beans

To garnish: Leaves of a bunch spearmint, chopped
1 bunch fresh parsley, chopped

NUTRITIONAL INFORMATION:
Energy (calories): 278kcal
Carbohydrates: 47.65 g
Protein: 14.04g
Fats: 4.59 g
Fiber: 11.1g

DIRECTIONS:

Soak beans overnight, strain and discard water. Place drained beans in a pot. Cover with water and place over medium heat. Bring to boil. After 5 minutes, strain and discard water. Return beans to pot, cover with water, bring to boil. Cook until tender. Water sauté all other ingredients except garnish herbs and add to the pot. Bring to a boil and simmer for 10 minutes. Add salt and pepper to taste. Garnish with spearmint and parsley. Ladle into soup bowls and enjoy.

Ramen Broth Base

Yield: 12 cups | Preparation Time: 15 minutes | Cooking Time: 2 hours

INGREDIENTS:

- 1 large onion, chopped
- 1 garlic bulb, chopped
- 4 sticks celery, chopped
- 1 Fuji apple (or any other kind you have), chopped
- 1 potato, peeled, chopped
- 6 cremini mushrooms, chopped
- 2 Tbsp. Himalayan pink salt
- 6 Nori sheets
- 3L water (12 cups)
- Salt and pepper to taste

DIRECTIONS:

Add all ingredients to a pot and simmer for 2 hours. Strain the broth and save the veggies to add to soups, stews, etc. to thicken. Transfer the stock to some jars. Let them cool before placing in the fridge. Use to add taste to any dish.

To make Ramen: Heat desired amount of broth to boil, add crushed garlic, soy sauce, chili flakes (optional). While it is boiling, grind 1 carrot, ground red cabbage, 1 tsp. fennel, 1 red pepper, sliced, 3 chopped scallions, 1 tsp. roasted sesame seeds and place it in a bowl with spiraled zucchini noodles. Pour broth over the ingredients and garnish with sprouts, basil leaves or lemongrass. Wait a few minutes for the flavors to blend. Serve and enjoy.

Slow Cooker All Purpose Vegetable Broth

Yield: 8 cups | Preparation Time: 10 minutes | Cooking Time: 6 hours

INGREDIENTS:

- 2 onions peeled and quartered
- 2 large carrots, peeled and cut into chunks
- 4 stalks celery, chopped
- 3 green peppers, seeded, chopped
- Other vegetable trimmings, optional
- 8 cups water
- 2 bay leaves
- 4 peppercorns
- 1 bunch of parsley
- 1 bunch of dill
- 2 leeks
- 2 Tbsp. salt or more to taste

Use the following as a guideline. Feel free to mix and match the vegetables according to what you have on hand and what you like. The idea is to boil vegetables and add spices you like.

DIRECTIONS:

Place all the vegetables and trimmings in the crock of a slow cooker. Add the water, bay leaf, peppercorns, and salt. Cover and cook 4 to 6 hours on High. Strain broth to use in recipes or freeze for later use.

To freeze: chill broth completely. Divide into 1 and 2 cup containers and freeze. Store in freezer until ready to use. This broth can be used in many dishes to give extra flavor. You will see it in many of the recipes in this book. Use in soups, stews, casseroles.

"So, whether you eat or drink, or whatever you do, do all to the glory of God."

1 Corinthians 10:31

Entreé Recipes

HOW TO BULID MY PARADISE GARDEN POWER BOWL

WHAT IS IT?

It is a yummy, delicious "all-in-one" layered meal that is packed with a variety of veggies, sprouts, beans, brown rice, etc. and topped off with grains, nuts, seeds and drizzled with your favorite sauce. You can create your own personalized bowl to enjoy all the savory flavors and textures that nature has to offer. Because of the combination of grains, greens and beans, you are getting a bowl full of complete proteins – all the essential amino acids that your body needs will be provided.

Here are some inspirational ideas to get you started. Keep in mind that it can be eaten anytime but during the fasting time, you may have to omit any ingredients that are not permitted during the fast. You can use as many or as few ingredients as you want to in your creation.

The idea is to create distinctive combinations of foods from around the world by blending the ingredients you like. You can create your own version of burrito bowl, open sushi bowl, teriyaki bowl, Indian biryani, and more! Be creative and enjoy. Choose the ingredients you like and mix in a bowl. Enjoy!

PICK YOUR BASE

Cooked Brown/Black/ Rice, Biryani, Quinoa, Lentils, Corn, Beans, Barley, Chickpeas, Buckwheat, Ancient Grains.

PICK YOUR CHOPPED /SHREDDED VEGGIE

Kale, Romaine, Bok Choy, Spinach, Zucchini, Cabbage, Mushrooms, Carrots, Cucumbers, Mixed Greens, Sprouts, Artichoke, Avocado, Peppers, Broccoli, Green Onions, Radish, Watercress, Tomatoes, Red Onion, Cauliflower, Red Pepper, Avocado, Edamame, Green Peas, Leaks, Sprouted Beans, Bamboo Shoots, Peas, Lentils.

PICK YOUR ROASTED VEGGIES

Red, Green/Yellow Bell Pepper, Cabbage, Mushrooms, Eggplant, Red Potatoes, Sweet Potato, Summer Squash, Turnips, Parsnips, Beets, Broccoli, Cauliflower, Snow Peas, Green Beans, Butternut Squash, Pumpkin, Okra, Zucchini, Soybeans, Edamame, Lima Beans, Jalapeno Peppers.

PICK YOUR SEEDS AND NUTS (PRE-SOAKED OR ROASTED)

Chia Seeds, Flaxseed, Hemp Seeds, Poppy Seed, Pumpkin Seeds, Sesame Seeds, Safflower, Sunflower, Almond, Walnut, Brazil Nut, Mustard Seeds, Cashew, Chestnuts, Hazelnut, Pine Nut, Macadamia, Pistachio, Pecan.

Peanut Sauce, Tahini-Lemon, Hummus, Pesto, Pico De Gallo, Vinegar-Olive Oil, Balsamic Vinegar, Apple Cider Vinegar, Mint and Coriander Chutney, Curry Sauce, Hot Sauce, Ginger–Garlic, Limes, Orange, Mustard, Garlic Lemon Sauce, Tamarind, Tomato Sauce, Balsamic or Apple Cider Vinegar, Raw Coconut Vinegar, Miso Dip, Ginger-Lime, Tahini Dip With Avocado, Carrot Miso, Salsa, Guacamole, Spinach Artichoke Dip, Vegan Buffalo Chicken Wing Dip, Baba Ganoush, Chili Mango Dipping Sauce, Hummus, Sweet Potato Coconut Dip, Artichoke Dip, Olive Tapenade.

PICK YOUR SEASONINGS

Salt, Black Pepper, Curry, Garlic Powder, Cloves, Onion Powder, Turmeric, Curry, Garam Masala, Chili Powder, Smoked Jalapeño Peppers, Teriyaki Sauce, Mustard, Thyme, Cayenne Pepper, Red Pepper, Ginger, Mint, Dill, Oregano, Basil, Cilantro, Parsley, Chives, Rosemary, Cumin, Bragg Organic Sprinkle, Adobo.

How to Assemble the Bowl

LAYERING METHOD:
Layer all ingredients in the bowl. This method is best used when you want a grab and go meal. Keep the dressing in a separate container to place on the meal just before you eat it. Great for taking with you for lunch, dinner, etc.

CLOCKWISE METHOD:
Place the grains/starch in the bottom of the bowl. Then place a small pile of your chopped vegetables, nuts, etc. in a circle clockwise making a colorful arrangement. Drizzle with your sauce or dressing and garnish. Enjoy.

SALAD METHOD:
Place all ingredients in a bowl. Mix with dressing or sauce.

Quinoa Veggie Bowl

Servings: 4 | Amount per Serving: 380 g 13.4 oz.
Preparation Time: 15 minutes | Cooking Time: 25 minutes

INGREDIENTS:

- 6 oz. (180 g) uncooked quinoa
- 2 cups water
- A pinch salt
- 4 avocado, peeled, pitted and sliced
- 4 celery stalk, diced
- 12 oz. mushrooms, sliced
- 2 tbsp. flaxseeds oil
- 4 cup arugula
- 1 tsp. dried oregano

NUTRITIONAL INFORMATION:
Energy (calories): 407kcal
Carbohydrates: 24.43 g
Protein: 8.63g
Fats: 34.74 g
Fiber: 16.1g

DIRECTIONS:

Bring a saucepan of water to a boil over medium heat and add the quinoa. Cover and let the quinoa simmer for 10 to 15 minutes until the water is completely absorbed and the quinoa is fluffy. Drain the quinoa and transfer to a bowl to cool. In the meantime, water sauté the mushrooms until the liquid evaporates (just a couple of minutes). Once the quinoa has cooled, stir in the avocado, cooked mushrooms and arugula making sure that it is mixed well. Season and serve.

Paradise Garden Asian Bowl

Servings: 4 | Amount per Serving: 500g or 16.6 oz.
Preparation Time: 10 minutes | Cooking Time: 35 minutes

INGREDIENTS:

- 20 oz. of quinoa, cooked
- 1 medium red bell pepper, thinly sliced
- 1 lbs. of chickpeas, cooked
- 4 cups of lettuce salad, shredded
- 2 medium cucumber, thinly sliced
- 1 avocado, thinly sliced
- 1 Tbsp. of alfalfa sprouts
- 1 tsp. of toasted sesame seeds

Asian Dressing:
- 2 Tbsp. of peanut butter
- Juice of 1 lemon
- 2 Tbsp. of olive oil
- 2 Tbsp. of water
- Salt & black pepper to taste

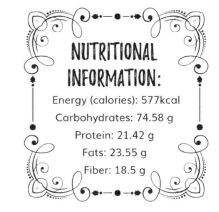

NUTRITIONAL INFORMATION:
Energy (calories): 577kcal
Carbohydrates: 74.58 g
Protein: 21.42 g
Fats: 23.55 g
Fiber: 18.5 g

DIRECTIONS:

Begin by preheating your oven to 400°F. Toss the cooked chickpeas and peppers with bit of oil and salt. Spread on a baking tray and roast in the oven for 20 to 25 minutes. Meanwhile, whisk the ingredients for the dressing in a bowl, until the peanut butter is thoroughly mixed in. Arrange the remaining ingredients in a bowl with the cooked quinoa, add the vegetables, and roasted chickpeas, drizzle with the satay dressing and top with toasted sesame seeds.

Raw Pad Thai Bowl

Servings: 4 | Amount per Serving: 550g or 19 oz.
Preparation Time: 20 minutes

INGREDIENTS:

- 4 zucchinis, thin strips
- 4 cups bean sprouts
- 2 red & yellow bell peppers, sliced into strips
- 8 green onions, diced
- 1 cup fresh cilantro, chopped
- 2 lime, juiced
- 2 tbsp. olive oil
- 1/2 tsp. sea salt
- 3/4 cup nuts (optional)

NUTRITIONAL INFORMATION:
Energy (calories): 425kcal
Carbohydrates: 27.52 g
Protein: 14.09g
Fats: 34.02 g
Fiber: 9g

DIRECTIONS:

Combine the zucchini strips, bean sprouts, bell pepper strips, green onions, and cilantro in a large bowl. Drizzle with fresh lime juice and olive oil. Sprinkle with sea salt and seasonings. Test and adjust seasonings to you taste. Top with chopped or crushed nuts or seeds. Serve and enjoy!

Hawaiian Garden Bowl

Servings: 4 | Amount per Serving: 420g or 14oz
Preparation Time: 10 minutes | Cooking Time: 15 minutes

INGREDIENTS:

- 5 oz. brown rice
- 5 oz. millet
- 4 tbsp. sushi vinegar
- 2 avocados
- 1 mango
- 8 radishes, sliced
- 1 cucumber, sliced
- 2 cups of baby spinach
- 2 oz. red cabbage (piece)
- 3 tbsp. black and white mixed sesame seeds
- 4 tbsp. Japanese soy sauce
- 1 lime juice
- 1 fresh red chili pepper to taste (or dried ground red pepper)
- 4 tbsp. sesame oil

NUTRITIONAL INFORMATION:
Energy (calories): 680kcal
Carbohydrates: 83.45 g
Protein: 13.38 g
Fat: 35.18g
Fiber 14.8g

DIRECTIONS:

Directions: Cook the rice and millet according to the instructions on the packages. Sprinkle the rice with sushi vinegar during the (15 min.) cooking process. Meanwhile, make the dressing: mix all ingredients. Remove the seeds from the red pepper and cut the flesh into thin strips. Cut the mango into cubes, and radishes, cucumber and avocado, drizzled with lime juice. Shave the red cabbage very thin and put the spinach in cold water. Divide the cooled rice and millet into four bowls and arrange the vegetables and mango all around. Divide the spinach leaves on top of each bowl. Serve the bowls with the soy dressing and sprinkle with mixed sesame seeds.

Indiana Succotash

Servings: 4 | Amount per Serving: 420g or 14 oz.
Preparation Time: 5 minutes | Cooking Time: 25 minutes

INGREDIENTS:

- 2 lbs. green beans
- 6 green onions with tops, chopped
- 1 red pepper, diced
- 18 oz. whole kernel corn, frozen
- 4 oz. lentils, sprouted and cooked
- 1 tsp. salt
- 4 tbsp. of sesame oil
- 1/4 tsp. paprika
- 1/4 tsp. celery salt

NUTRITIONAL INFORMATION:

Energy (calories): 300kcal

Carbohydrates: 37.06 g

Protein: 8.46g

Fats: 16.81 g

Fiber: 7.8g

DIRECTIONS:

Directions: Cut beans in rounds the size of corn, cook with 1 tsp. salt about 15 minutes or until tender, drain. Water sauté green onions and red pepper until transparent (do not brown). Add corn, sprouted lentils, paprika, celery salt, and beans. Simmer succotash, covered, for about 10 more minutes.

Sweet Potato Bowl

Servings: 4 | Amount per Serving: 350 g or 11.6 oz.
Preparation Time: 10 minutes

INGREDIENTS:

- 4 sweet potatoes, baked
- 2 cup green beans, steamed
- 1 cup Edamame, steamed
- 1 cup peas, steamed
- 2 avocados, chopped into chunks
- 4 tsp. of sunflower and hemp seeds mixed together

Dressing:
- 4 tbsp. lime juice
- 1 tsp. Tahini
- Salt and pepper

NUTRITIONAL INFORMATION:

Energy (calories): 234 kcal

Carbohydrates: 41.2 g

Protein: 8.34 g

Fats: 5.88 g

Fiber: 7.4 g

DIRECTIONS:

Mix the cooked Edamame, peas and avocado chunks with lime juice, salt and pepper. Mix well. Cut the baked potatoes in half and fill it with edamame and peas mixture. Place the green beans in the bowl next to the potatoes. Mix dressing, adjust the spices (add water to liquefy, if necessary). Drizzle over the veggies. Sprinkle with seeds and dressing.

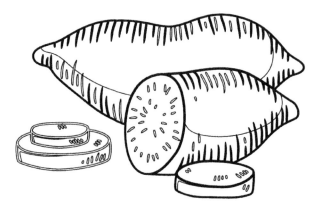

Spicy Quinoa Veggie Bowl

Servings: 4 | Amount per Serving: 440 g or 14.6 oz.
Preparation Time: 15 minutes | Cooking Time: 30 minutes

INGREDIENTS:

- 3.5 oz. Edamame beans, shelled
- 3 tbsp. toasted sesame oil

Quinoa and rest of the Vegetables
- 2 cups water
- 3.5 oz. quinoa
- ½ tsp. fine sea salt
- 1 lbs. butternut squash, skin off, diced
4 tbsp. of sesame seeds, roasted

- ¼ tsp. dried chili flakes
- 1 lime, juice only
- 3.5 oz. bok choi, cut in lengths (1 inch wide)
- 10 cherry tomatoes, halved
- 1 avocado, sliced
- 2 spring onions, thinly sliced
4 tbsp. of sesame seeds, roasted

NUTRITIONAL INFORMATION:

Energy (calories): 401kcal

Carbohydrates: 38.8 g

Protein: 10.53 g

Fats: 25.42 g

Fiber: 10 g

DIRECTIONS:

Preheat the oven to 400 degrees F. Place the butternut squash cubes into a large mixing bowl and mix with sesame oil and lime juice. Spread the squash out evenly across the baking sheet lined with parchment paper. Sprinkle the squash with salt, black and chili pepper. Roast the squash for 20-30 minutes, stirring once halfway through and continue cooking until the largest pieces of squash are tender. Transfer it to the mixing bowl. In the meantime, cook quinoa according to the package instructions and transfer into a mixing bowl. Steam the Edamame beans. Bring about an inch of water to a boil in a pot. Put the Edamame in a colander or a steam basket. Once the water is boiling, add the vessel to the pot, cover, and steam the Edamame until they are heated through and tender, 5 to 10 minutes. Remove from the pot and transfer the Edamame into a mixing bowl with cooked quinoa and roasted squash. Heat water in a skillet and shortly water sauté the bok choi, for a minute or two. Add it to the bowl. Halve the avocado and remove the pit. Thinly slice the flesh and add it to the mixing bowl too, cut the tomatoes and spring onion and combine it with the rest of the ingredients. Before serving sprinkle it with sesame seeds and serve.

Opa Greek Paradise Garden Bowl

Servings: 4 | Amount per Serving: 460 g or 15.3 oz.
Preparation Time: 10 minutes | Cooking Time: 20 minutes

INGREDIENTS:

- 30 oz. of cooked chickpeas
- 2 Tbsp. of avocado oil
- 2 Tbsp. Shawarma Spice Blend
- 1/2 tsp. sea salt

Bowl
- 4 Tbsp. chopped parsley
- 2 cups green or Kalamata olives, pitted
- 1 cup cherry tomatoes, halved
- 2 medium cucumber, thinly sliced
- 3 medium carrots

NUTRITIONAL INFORMATION:

Energy (calories): 530 kcal

Carbohydrates: 71.23 g

Protein: 20.88 g

Fats: 20.38 g

Fiber: 20.9 g

DIRECTIONS:

Preheat oven to 375 degrees F (190 C) and set out a baking sheet. Add washed, dried chickpeas to a mixing bowl along with oil, Shawarma Spice Blend, and salt. Toss to combine. Add seasoned chickpeas to the baking sheet. Bake for 20-23 minutes or until the chickpeas are slightly crispy and golden brown. Remove from oven and set aside. Assemble bowl by dividing olives, tomatoes, cucumber, and carrots parsley, (optional) between four serving bowls. Top with cooked chickpeas and garnish with fresh lemon juice.

Korean Paradise Veggie Bowl

Servings: 4 | Preparation Time: 15 minutes | Cooking Time: 30 minutes

INGREDIENTS:

For the Quinoa
• 2 cups water
• 3 ½ oz. quinoa
• ½ tsp. sea salt

For Vegetables
• 4 oz. Edamame beans or pea beans, frozen, shelled
• 3 scallions, chopped on a diagonal
• 1 carrot, sliced-strips, roll to look like a smoked salmon
• 2 Tbsp. arame, finely shredded
• 1 avocado, pitted, peeled, sliced.
• 3 Tbsp. toasted sesame oil
• ¼ tsp. dried chili flakes
• 1 Tbsp. kimchi or pickles
• 2 Tbsp. mango

Garnish: Lemongrass or ½ -1 lime, juice (optional)

For mushrooms:
• 1 cup Shitake mushrooms
• ½ Tbsp. oil
• ½ Tbsp. ginger, minced
• 2 Tbsp. soy sauce
• Salt and pepper
• ½ tsp. red chili, flakes (optional)
• For the Marinated Baked Tempeh
• 1 (8-ounce) package tempeh into triangles for grilling or sliced on diagonal for baking

For Marinate
• ¼ cup soy sauce
• 2 Tbsp. rice vinegar
• 1 date
• 1 Tbsp. extra-virgin olive oil
• 1 teaspoon sriracha
• Freshly ground black pepper
• ½ Tbsp. ginger, minced (optional)

DIRECTIONS:

Cover arame with filtered water and soak for about 15 minutes. Drain and set aside. To Cook the Shitake mushrooms: with oil and ginger.

For Baked or Grilled Tempeh: In order the tempeh to become tender, pre-cut and steam for 10 minutes. Blend the marinade. Place the tempeh in a shallow dish and pour the marinade on top to coat. Marinate for at least 30 minutes. Preheat the oven to 425°F and line a baking sheet with oiled parchment paper. Arrange the sliced tempeh onto the baking sheet, reserving the excess marinade. Bake 10 minutes. Remove from the oven and brush more of the marinade onto the cubes. Bake 10 more minutes or until the cubes are charred around the edges.

For grilled tempeh: Cut the tempeh into triangles and follow the marinating instructions above. Grill the tempeh 5-10 minutes on the first side. Remove from grill. Dip it back into the marinade to coat and then return it to the grill. Gill the second side for 4-5 minutes, or until deep char marks form.

To Assemble the Bowl: Place the quinoa in the bottom of the bowl. Then place each pile of chopped vegetables, mushrooms and tempeh in the bowl in a circle clockwise making a colorful arrangement. Drizzle with the extra marinade, sesame oil, sesame seeds and squeeze of lime. Enjoy.

Garlic Chickpea Burger

Servings: 4 | Amount per Serving: 300g or 10oz.
Preparation Time: 15 minutes | Resting Time: 30 minutes
Cooking Time: 25 minutes

INGREDIENTS:

- 1 tsp. cumin
- 1 cup cilantro, fresh chopped
- 6 tbsp. of flaxseeds, ground, plus more for rolling
- 4 tbsp. water for sauté
- 2 onions, chopped
- 3 cloves garlic, minced
- 2 lbs. chickpeas, cooked
- 1 tsp. paprika
- 1 tsp. coriander powder

NUTRITIONAL INFORMATION:

Energy (calories): 535kcal
Carbohydrates: 59.71g
Protein: 18.98g
Fats: 26.7 g
Fiber: 19.2 g

DIRECTIONS:

Finely chop the onions and crush the garlic and add to a frying pan and water sauté until just before they start to brown. Drain the can of chickpeas and add the chickpeas to a food processor with the cooked onions/garlic, paprika, coriander powder, cumin, freshly chopped cilantro and flaxseeds and process it into a thick burger batter. Sprinkle a bit more flaxseeds over a baking tray and cover your hands with it as well. Scoop the batter out onto the tray in 4 even sections, roll in the flax and form into 4 balls.

If the batter is very sticky or too wet, add more flax so that it easily forms a ball. Take a square of parchment paper, place on top of each ball and press down on it with the bottom of a glass to flatten it into a burger shape. Place the baking tray with the 4 burgers into the freezer to firm up for 30 minutes. After 30 minutes place on a parchment lined baking tray and bake in the oven at 400°F (200°C) for a further 30-40 minutes until done. Serve with Watercress and lettuce salad with seeds.

Black Bean Hummus Burrito

Servings: 4 | Amount per Serving: : 610g or 21.5oz
Preparation Time: 10 minutes | Cooking Time: 15 minutes

INGREDIENTS:

- 2 onions, chopped
- 2 bell pepper, chopped
- 8 oz. sliced mushrooms
- 1 can corn, rinsed, drained 480g
- 16 oz. roasted red bell pepper hummus
- 4 large whole red lentil flatbread
- 1 14 oz. can black beans, rinsed and drained
- 2 roasted Poblano pepper, cut into strips
- 1 package (10 oz.) fresh spinach

DIRECTIONS:

Preheat oven to 450 F. Water sauté the onion until translucent. Add the bell pepper and cook for 2 to 3 minutes. Add the mushrooms and corn. Spread a layer of hummus on the red lentil flatbread. Add the sautéed vegetables, beans, Poblano strips, and fresh spinach. Roll into a burrito. Serve the wrap warm, and top with guacamole and salsa.

Lettuce Wraps with Quinoa

Servings: 4 | Amount per Serving:120g or 4.2 oz.
Preparation Time: 10 minutes | Cooking Time: 10 minutes

INGREDIENTS:

- 3$^{1/2}$ tbsp. uncooked quinoa
- 12 tbsp. black beans
- 12 tbsp. canned corn
- 4 tbsp. fresh parsley, chopped
- 4 green onion, cut into rings
- 8 lettuce leaves, medium

NUTRITIONAL INFORMATION:

Energy (calories): 238kcal
Carbohydrates: 45.13 g
Protein: 9.02g
Fats: 2.99 g
Fiber: 7.3g

DIRECTIONS:

Cook the quinoa according to the instructions on the package. Rinse and drain the black beans and the corn. In a medium-sized bowl, combine the green onion black beans and the corn with cooked quinoa. Equally fill the quinoa mixture into the lettuce leaves and top them with chipotle sauce (See recipe in Dips Dressings and Sauces section). Serve.

Jackfruit Lentil Wraps

Servings: 4 | Amount per Serving: 370 g or 12.3 oz.
Preparation Time: 10 minutes | Cooking Time: 10 minutes

INGREDIENTS:

- 1 cup red lentils, cooked
- 2 cups water
- ½ tsp. salt
- ½ tsp. of garam masala
- 1 can jackfruit ~13.6 oz. -15oz.
- 1 pack of Schwartz Mexican Seasoning
- 1 small green pepper, chopped
- 1 small red pepper, chopped
- Choice of Lettuce or red lentil flatbread, for wrapping
- 3 Tbsp. Cannellini Mayo Dressing
- 1 lime, juice
- 1 ripe avocado, pitted, peeled

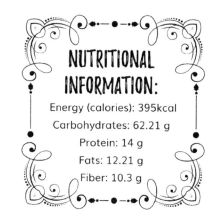

NUTRITIONAL INFORMATION:
Energy (calories): 395kcal
Carbohydrates: 62.21 g
Protein: 14 g
Fats: 12.21 g
Fiber: 10.3 g

DIRECTIONS:

Water sauté jackfruit with peppers, lime juice and spices for 5 minutes, until done. Place jackfruit on the wraps and layer with lentils, avocado and seasonings. Wrap like a burrito and enjoy.

Lentil Taco Wrap with Pico de Gallo

Servings: 4 | Amount per Serving: 200g or 6.6 oz.
Preparation Time: 10 minutes | Cooking Time: 30 minutes

NUTRITIONAL INFORMATION:
Energy (calories): 278kcal
Carbohydrates: 29.08 g
Protein: 4.7g
Fats: 16.5 g
Fiber: 5.2g

INGREDIENTS:

- 4-8 Lettuce leaves for wrapping
- ½ cup brown lentils, dried
- 1 ¼ - 1 ½ cups veggie broth
- 1 medium white onion, chopped
- 1 large red/green pepper, chopped
- 2 small garlic cloves, minced
- 3 tbsp. avocado oil
- 1 ½ tbsp. taco seasoning
- 1 tsp. lime juice
- Salt & pepper to taste

DIRECTIONS:

First, dice all the veggies and rinse the lentils to remove any debris. Then, add the veggie broth, lentils, and ½ tbsp. of the taco seasoning to a small saucepan. Cook the lentils uncovered for 25-30 minutes until they are soft. Check and stir periodically to make sure the lentils are not getting overcooked. Start with 1 ¼ cup vegetable broth and add up to ¼ cup more broth if the lentils are sticking to the pan before cooked through. The lentils are done when they are slightly crunchy on the outside (not mushy!), soft and tender inside, and no liquid is left in the pan. Salt and pepper to taste. While the lentils are cooking, add 1 tbsp. of oil to a large pan or cast iron skillet and turn the heat on. Once the oil is hot, add in the chopped onion, garlic, red/green pepper, and 1 tbsp. of taco seasoning. Water sauté for 5 minutes until the vegetables are cooked, but still crispy. Then, turn off the heat and season with salt and pepper to taste. Add the cooked lentils to the skillet with vegetables and 1 tsp. of lime juice. Stir to mix everything together. Then, fill each lettuce leaf with the lentil taco filling and add Avocado Pico de Gallo sauce over each tortilla.

Roasted Red Pepper Tapenade Sandwich with Alfalfa Sprouts

Servings: 4 | Amount per Serving: 400 g or 14.1 oz.
Preparation Time: 5 minutes | Cooking Time: 15 minutes

INGREDIENTS:

- 4 thick slices of Gluten Free Quinoa + Chia Bread
- 4 tbsp. roasted red pepper hummus
- 2 large carrot, peeled and finely grated
- 2 cucumbers, sliced
- 2 avocado, peeled, halved, and sliced lengthwise
- 2 cups alfalfa sprouts
- Pinch sea salt and ground pepper to taste.

NUTRITIONAL INFORMATION:

Energy (calories): 238kcal

Carbohydrates: 45.13 g

Protein: 9.02g

Fats: 2.99 g

Fiber: 7.3g

DIRECTIONS:

Spread hummus on each bread slice and place carrot, cucumber, and avocado on top of each bread slices. Sprinkle it with alfalfa sprout and serve.

Baked Falafel Burgers

Servings: 4 | Amount per Serving: 300 g or 10 oz.
Preparation Time: 10 minutes | Cooking Time: 50 minutes

INGREDIENTS:

- 3 cups fresh parsley, chopped
- 6 cloves garlic
- 1 large lemon, juiced
- 1/2 tsp. each sea salt & black pepper
- 1 1/4 tsp. cumin
- 30 oz. of cooked chickpeas
- 1 cup raw walnuts, ground

NUTRITIONAL INFORMATION:

Energy (calories): 530 kcal

Carbohydrates: 71.23 g

Protein: 20.88 g

Fats: 20.38 g

Fiber: 20.9 g

DIRECTIONS:

Preheat oven to 375 degrees F. Add parsley, garlic, lemon juice, cumin, and a healthy pinch each salt and pepper to a food processor and mix to combine. Add chickpeas and pulse until incorporated but still slightly chunky. You want to maintain a bit of texture. Transfer to a mixing bowl and add ground walnuts and mix again until a loose dough is formed that's firm enough to be handled. Taste and adjust seasonings as needed. Add a touch more salt.

Draw an "x" in the dough to form 4 sections, then use your hands to form into 4 large patties roughly 1/2-inch thick. Place on a foil-lined baking sheet and refrigerate or freeze for 15 minutes to firm up. Bake for a total of 30-40 minutes, flipping once at the halfway point for even cooking. The longer you bake them, the firmer they'll get! Serve warm with tomato and cucumber salad.

Spicy Black Bean Burger

Servings: 4 | Amount per Serving: 280g or 9.3 oz.
Preparation Time: 10 minutes | Cooking Time: 15 minutes

INGREDIENTS:

- 30 oz. cooked black beans
- ½ cup pumpkin flour
- ¼ cup flaxseeds
- ½ cup oats flour
- ½ cup salsa
- 2 tsp. cumin, ground
- 1 tsp. garlic salt

NUTRITIONAL INFORMATION:
Energy (calories): 488kcal
Carbohydrates: 67.04 g
Protein: 27.8g
Fats: 14.29 g
Fiber: 23.9g

DIRECTIONS:

Place beans in food processor and process them until they are fairly smooth. Add pumpkin flour, oats and flax, salsa, cumin and garlic salt. Process until well combined. Spoon the mixture into 4 balls on a large plate and refrigerate at least 1 hour or up to 4 hours before cooking. Heat barbecue grill or ridged grill pan over medium heat. Coat grill or pan lightly with oil. Form each ball into a 4-inch-wide patty about 1/2-inch thick. Place the patties on the grill or in a pan and then cook until browned and heated through. This should take about 4 to 5 minutes per side. Serve.

Bean Burger Patties

Servings: 4 | Amount per Serving: 230 g or 7.6 oz.
Preparation Time: 15 minutes | Cooking Time: 10 minutes

INGREDIENTS:

- 3 cups black beans, cooked
- 4 cloves garlic
- 4 scallions, roughly chopped
- 1/2 cup walnuts
- 1 cup old fashioned rolled oats
- 1/2 tsp. chili powder
- 1/2 tsp. smoked paprika
- 1 Tbsp. of tamari sauce
- 1 Tbsp. red wine vinegar
- 4 Tbsp. of sesame seeds
- 4 Tbsp. oil for cooking

NUTRITIONAL INFORMATION:
Energy (calories): 571 kcal
Carbohydrates: 61.48 g
Protein: 21.8 g
Fats: 28.55 g
Fiber: 17.7 g

DIRECTIONS:

Add the garlic to the bowl of a food processor and pulse until finely minced. Add the scallions, and then pulse until chopped small. Scrape down the sides, and then add the oats, walnuts, chili powder, smoked paprika, tamari, red wine vinegar. Process it into a fine texture that looks like breadcrumbs. Measure about 1/2 cup of the black beans and set it aside. Add the remaining black beans to the food processor. Pulse until mostly smooth with some texture. Scrape the mixture into a bowl and fold in the reserved 1/2 cup of beans. Set the mixture aside for 5 minutes so that the oats have a chance to absorb any excess moisture in the mixture. When you are ready to make the burgers, divide into 4 equal portions patties. Form each portion into a round patty, firmly molding and pressing the mixture together so that it does not fall apart. Heat a skillet over medium-low heat, and then place patties in one layer. Bake at 375°F for 20 minutes or until done. Serve.

Mexican Green Chili Veggie Burgers

Servings: 4 | Amount per Serving: 220 g or 7.3 oz.
Preparation Time: 5 minutes | Cooking Time: 20 minutes

INGREDIENTS:

- 2 medium shallots, minced
- 3 cloves garlic, minced
- 20 oz. chickpeas, cooked
- 1-2 Tbsp. avocado oil
- 1 4-oz. can mild green chilis
- 1 tsp. cumin
- 1 tsp. chili powder
- 1 medium lime
- 1 cup of fresh cilantro, finely chopped
- 1/2 cup flaxseeds, ground
- 1 tsp. of sea salt and pepper (to taste)

NUTRITIONAL INFORMATION:

Energy (calories): 412 kcal

Carbohydrates: 49.57 g

Protein: 17.21 g

Fats: 18.12 g

Fiber: 17.7 g

DIRECTIONS:

Heat a large skillet over medium heat (and preheat oven to 375 degrees F (190 C) for a firmer burger). Line a baking sheet with parchment paper or leave bare. Once skillet is hot, add 1 Tbsp. oil, shallot and garlic. Water sauté, stirring frequently, until soft and translucent - about 1-2 minutes. Add garlic and shallot directly to a mixing bowl. Then add drained chickpeas and use a fork or pastry cutter to mash/mix. Add remaining ingredients, including oil and stir/mash to combine. You want it to form into a moldable "dough." Add more oil or lime juice if too dry, or more crushed chips if too wet. Divide into 4 even patties. Place them on a baking sheet and bake in a 375° F (190 C) oven for 20-25 minutes or more until cooked. The longer you bake them, the drier/firmer they'll become. Let cool for 2-3 minutes before serving (they'll firm up as they cool). Serve with Avocado Salad and Red Lentil Flatbread.

Meat Free Meatballs

Servings: 4 | Amount per Serving: 180g g or 6 oz.
Preparation Time: 15 minutes | Cooking Time: 45 minutes

INGREDIENTS:

- 6 oz. cooked and cooled quinoa
- 2 cans black beans, drained
- 2 tbsp. water
- 3 cloves garlic, minced
- 1 tsp. onion powder
- ¼ tsp. sea salt
- 2½ tsp. fresh oregano
- ½ tsp. red pepper flakes
- ½ tsp. fennel seeds, optional
- 1 tsp. cumin powder
- 2 tbsp. tomato paste
- 3 tbsp. chopped fresh basil

NUTRITIONAL INFORMATION:

Energy (calories): 216kcal

Carbohydrates: 39.36 g

Protein: 12.66 g

Fats: 1.6 g

Fiber: 12 g

DIRECTIONS:

Begin by preheating your oven to 350°F. Mix all ingredients until it is like a dough. Form into small meatballs and bake in oven on a baking pan lined with oiled parchment paper for about 20 minutes until they are cooked.

Spicy Roasted Chickpea Lettuce Wraps

Servings: 4 | Amount per Serving: 320g or 10.6 oz.
Preparation Time: 15 minutes | Cooking Time: 10 minutes

INGREDIENTS:

- 16 oz. cooked chickpeas
- 3 Tbsp. avocado oil or any oil with a high smoke point
- 1 tsp. curry
- 1/2 tsp. cumin
- 1/4 tsp. cayenne pepper (less if you're heat sensitive)
- 1/2 tsp. ground sea salt
- Ground black pepper to taste
- 8 large leafs of romaine lettuce, washed and dried completely
- 2 carrots, peeled and spiralized or finely grated
- 1 green bell pepper, seeded and finely chopped
- 1 cup of walnuts, lightly toasted
- 12 cherry tomatoes, sliced thin
- 8 stalks of cilantro
- 1 lime, juiced

NUTRITIONAL INFORMATION:

Energy (calories): 457kcal

Carbohydrates: 44.17 g

Protein: 14.95g

Fats: 26.97 g

Fibers: 12.7g

DIRECTIONS:

Heat a skillet on medium heat and add the chickpeas. Roast for a few minutes then add the spices and stir until completely coated. Stir frequently and cook for approximately ten minutes or until the beans are crisp on the outside but still creamy on the inside. Put the walnuts in the pan a few minutes before the chickpeas are finished cooking to toast them. Spoon the chickpeas and walnuts into the lettuce leaves and top with the carrots, pepper, tomato, cilantro, and lime juice. Be liberal with the lime, it makes the dish.

BBQ Jackfruit Sandwiches

NUTRITIONAL INFORMATION:

Energy (calories): 719kcal

Carbohydrates: 156.76 g

Protein: 8.25 g

Fat: 9.12g

Fiber 9.5g

Servings: 4 | Amount per Serving: 500g or 16.6 oz.
Preparation Time: 5 minutes | Cooking Time: 10 minutes

INGREDIENTS:

- 8 oz. coleslaw mix
- 2 tsp. apple cider vinegar
- 3 tbsp. mayonnaise, homemade
- 40 oz. jackfruit about 2 cans, in water
- 2 tsp. dry barbecue rub
- 1 tbsp. avocado oil
- 1 cup barbecue sauce, homemade (120g)
- Salt
- Black pepper
- Flourless Nut Seed Bread, sliced
- Pickles sliced

DIRECTIONS:

Mix together the vinegar, coleslaw mix, mayonnaise, 1/2 tsp. salt, and a few pinches of pepper in a bowl. Cover with plastic wrap and refrigerate until ready to serve. Drain and seed jackfruit. Pull apart with two forks or use a hand mixer on low to break apart. Add the BBQ rub, 1/2 tsp. salt, and 1/2 tsp. pepper to the jackfruit and combine. In a baking pan lined with oiled parchment paper, place the jackfruit and cover with BBQ sauce and bake about 20 minutes at 375°F or until tender. Place the BBQ jackfruit on the sliced nut bread and serve with coleslaw and pickles.

Peas Potato Stew

Servings: 4 | Amount per Serving: 590g or 20.8 oz.
Preparation Time: 10 minutes | Cooking Time: 15 minutes

NUTRITIONAL INFORMATION:
Energy (calories): 367kcal
Carbohydrates: 37.33 g
Protein: 9.68 g
Fat: 21.76 g
Fiber 12.7g

INGREDIENTS:

- 6 tbsp. olive oil, divided
- 1 medium onion, chopped
- 2 leeks, chopped
- 2 potatoes, peeled, diced
- 4 garlic cloves, chopped
- 1 cup tomatoes, diced
- 6 cups frozen or fresh peas
- 1 carrot medium, chopped
- 1 ½ tsp. of dried dill, seasoning
- 1 tsp. paprika
- 1 tsp. smoke paprika
- 1 bay leaf
- 1 tsp. Italian spice
- Salt and pepper to taste
- ½ cup water or veggie broth

DIRECTIONS:

In a cooking pot add onion, tomatoes, garlic, water, spices and salt. Bring to boil. Turn down heat and simmer on low for 15-20 minutes. Add potato and carrots and simmer until potatoes are cooked. As leeks, peas and cook for 5 minutes more. Add water if too thick. Garnish with fresh dill. Serve.

Moroccan Vegetable Stew

Servings: 4 | Amount per Serving: 600g or 20 oz.
Preparation Time: 10 minutes | Cooking Time: 30 minutes

NUTRITIONAL INFORMATION:
Energy (calories): 271kcal
Carbohydrates: 50.62 g
Protein: 11.4g
Fats: 4.72 g
Fiber: 12.9g

INGREDIENTS:

- 2 cups chickpeas, cooked
- ½ Tbsp. olive oil
- 1 onion, chopped
- 1 red bell pepper, chopped
- 1 small jalapeno pepper, chopped
- ½ cup celery, chopped
- ½ cup carrots, chopped
- 2 cups mushrooms, sliced
- 3 cups vegetable broth
- 28 oz. can tomatoes, crushed
- 3 Tbsp. of raisins
- 1 Tbsp. apple juice, fresh
- ¼ tsp. ginger, ground
- ¼ tsp. coriander, ground
- 1/8 tsp. white pepper, ground
- 1/8 tsp. ground cinnamon
- Pinch of allspice and turmeric, ground
- Salt and pepper to taste

DIRECTIONS:

Place all ingredients except raisins and apple juice in a slow cooker and cook for 2 hours on low. Turn off. Stir in raisins, and juice. Serve.

Tuscany Zucchini, Noodles

Servings: 4 | Preparation Time: 10 minutes | Cooking Time: 5 minutes

INGREDIENTS:

- 4 large zucchinis, spiralized
For the sauce
- 1 medium onion, finely chopped
- ½ cup sun-dried tomatoes, chopped
- 1 Tbsp. black olives, pitted
- ½ Tbsp. green olives, pitted
- 1/2 roasted pepper, sliced
- ½ tbsp. tomato paste, (optional)
- 1 cup fresh basil leaves

- 2 Tbsp. olive oil
- 4 cloves garlic, minced
- ½ tbs. lemon zest
- 1 tbs. lemon juice (optional)
- 1 tsp. Italian seasoning
- 1/2 tsp. sea salt
- 1/2 tsp. red chili flakes
- Cracked black pepper, to taste

NUTRITIONAL INFORMATION:

Energy (calories): 401kcal

Carbohydrates: 38.8 g

Protein: 10.53 g

Fats: 25.42 g

Fiber: 10 g

DIRECTIONS:

Spiralize your zucchini and set aside in colander or on paper towels so that any excess water is removed. In an oiled baking tray, add garlic and onions and roast at 400° F for 10 minutes. Meanwhile, chop all other ingredients, add spices and mix with onion and garlic. Add zucchini noodles, cook for about 10 more minutes until tender. Mix well. Season with cracked pepper, chili flakes, chopped basil and Italian Seasoning. Serve and enjoy!

Lazy Cabbage Rolls with Mung Beans

Servings: 4 | Amount per Serving: 370 g or 12.3 oz.
Preparation Time: 20 minutes | Cooking Time: 30 minutes

INGREDIENTS:

- 1 cup brown rice
- 1 cup split mung beans
- ½ head of cabbage
- 1 small onion, diced
- 1 cup of Kalamata olives
- 1 tsp. chili flakes

- ½ tsp. thyme
- 1 tsp. basil
- ¼ tsp. oregano
- Salt and pepper, to taste
- 25 oz. jar of tomato sauce, or your favorite homemade variety

NUTRITIONAL INFORMATION:

Energy (calories): 434kcal

Carbohydrates: 82.2 g

Protein: 10.4g

Fats: 5.68 g

Fiber: 15.7g

DIRECTIONS:

In a medium-sized pot, rinse your rice a couple times before combining it with the mung beans and three cups of water. Cover and bring to a boil, reducing it to a simmer until all the water has been absorbed (about 20 minutes). In the meantime, put a kettle of water on to boil. Thinly slice the cabbage, dice the onion and chop olives into small slices. Place the cabbage in a large metal mixing bowl, and pour the boiling water over it. Stir the cabbage around for 3-4 minutes, until the cabbage is a vibrant green and slightly softer, then drain the water from the cabbage. Squeeze hard with your hands to remove as much liquid as possible. Add the onion, olive, spices and rice and mung beans (once they've been cooked) and mix well. If you allow the mixture to cool slightly, you can use your hands to mix. Add salt and pepper to taste. Preheat the oven to 375°F (190°C). In a large glass baking dish, pour a small amount of the tomato sauce into the bottom, and spread to cover. Next take a handful of the cabbage mixture (around ¾ of a cup) and use your hands to form the mixture into a spherical or egg-shaped ball, and place it in the pan. Continue until you have used all the cabbage and rice mixture (you should have around 12 balls total). Pour the remaining sauce over the cabbage balls and put in the oven for around 30 minutes, until the sauce is bubbling slightly. Remove and serve hot.

Stuffed Bell Peppers with Mushrooms

Servings: 4 | Amount per Serving: 460g or 16.2 oz.
Preparation Time: 15 minutes | Cooking Time: 35 minutes

INGREDIENTS:

- 14 oz. mushrooms, diced
- 2 cup vegetable broth
- 10 oz. barley, pre-cooked
- 2 Tbsp. oil
- 1 tsp. cumin
- 8 bell peppers, small, tops cut off and deseeded

For the tomato sauce
- 2 (14 oz.) can tomatoes
- 2 Tbsp. tomato puree
- 2 Tbsp. ground coriander
- 4 Tbsp. olive oil
- 1 garlic clove, minced
- Salt and pepper to taste
- 4 Tbsp. of parsley, fresh, chopped

NUTRITIONAL INFORMATION:

Energy (calories): 579 kcal

Carbohydrates: 85.05 g

Protein: 13.64g

Fats: 23.09 g

Fiber: 22.5 g

DIRECTIONS:

Preheat the oven to 375°F. Bring the veggie broth to boil and add the pre-cooked barley. Cook for 5 minutes until soft. Drain. Heat a sauté pan with the oil. Gently water sauté the mushrooms for a couple of minutes. Mix in the barley and add cumin. Make the sauce by mixing together the plum tomatoes, purée, ground coriander, garlic, salt and pepper.

Stuff each pepper with the barley mix. Put in a small oven dish and pour over the sauce. Cook in the oven for 25 minutes, until soft but still holding their shape. Serve immediately. Garnish with parsley before serving. Serve with Green salad with Pomegranate Arils.

Chili Bean Stew

Servings: 4 | Amount per Serving: 500g or 17.6 oz.
Preparation Time: 10 minutes | Cooking Time: 50 minutes

INGREDIENTS:

- 12 oz. dried kidney beans, presoaked
- 4 Tbsp. olive oil
- 2 medium onions, chopped
- 2 medium red bell pepper, chopped
- 2 large celery stalk, chopped
- 4 garlic cloves, minced
- 2 bay leaves
- 2 tsp. chili powder
- 2 tsp. cumin, ground
- 4 cups water
- 7 oz. of canned diced tomatoes, pureed in processor
- ½ tsp. of cayenne pepper

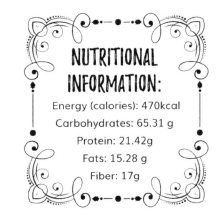

NUTRITIONAL INFORMATION:

Energy (calories): 470kcal

Carbohydrates: 65.31 g

Protein: 21.42g

Fats: 15.28 g

Fiber: 17g

DIRECTIONS:

Place beans in large bowl. Pour enough cold water over to cover beans by 2-inches. Let stand overnight. Drain. Heat the oil in heavy Dutch oven over medium-low heat. Add onion, bell pepper, celery, garlic and bay leaf; stir it to coat with oil. Cover and cook until vegetables are tender and light golden,

stirring occasionally, about 5 minutes. Uncover; add chili powder and cumin and stir again. Add beans, 3 cups water, tomatoes and cayenne; bring to boil. Reduce heat; cover and simmer until beans are tender, about 40 minutes. Uncover the stew; season to taste with salt and pepper. Serve.

Stuffed Bell Peppers with Zucchini, Mushrooms and Rice

Servings: 4 | Amount per Serving: 360g or 12 oz.
Preparation Time: 10 minutes | Cooking Time: 30 minutes

INGREDIENTS:

- ½ cup whole grain brown rice, uncooked
- 4 medium bell peppers, any color (red, yellow, or green)
- 3 Tbsp. olive oil
- 2 small onions, diced
- 2 cups crimini mushrooms, sliced
- 2 small carrots, sliced
- 1 medium zucchini, cubed
- 3/4 cup fresh parsley, leaves picked and finely chopped
- 3/4 cup tomato purée
- Salt, to taste
- Freshly ground black pepper, to taste
- A pinch of chili powder

DIRECTIONS:

Preheat the oven to 425 °F. In a small pan bring a salted water to a boil over medium heat and cook the rice according to the package instructions. Drain on a colander and set aside.Cut off the tops of the bell peppers (lids) and set aside. Scoop out the inside and discard the seeds. Wash the peppers carefully and set aside. In a large pan heat add little water, add onion and water sauté for 2-3 minutes until soft. Add the mushrooms and sauté for a further 5-8 minutes. Add carrots and zucchini, stirring occasionally for 5 minutes. Remove from the heat. Add cooked rice, 1/3 cup parsley, tomato purée, and stir until well combined. Season to taste with salt, pepper and a pinch of chili. Divide the mixture between the peppers and place the lids on top. Place the stuffed peppers in a greased baking tray. Bake for 20-25 minutes, until slightly brown on the edges. Sprinkle remaining parsley on top and serve.

Seaweed Congee "Chinese Rice Porridge"

Servings: 4-6 | Preparation Time: 15 minutes | Cooking Time: 10 minutes

INGREDIENTS:

- ½ cup short grain rice
- 1 inch piece fresh ginger, minced
- 2 cloves garlic, minced
- 7 dried shiitake mushrooms, soaked in hot water, chopped
- 5 cups water
- ½ small head Bok Choy, chopped
- 2-6" strip of dried Kombu

For Toppings:
Use any one or more
- 1 medium carrot, finely chopped
- 2 tbsp. scallions
- 1 Tbsp. seaweed-arame, finely shredded
- Salt or Dulse to taste
- 2 Tbsp. cashews or pumpkin seeds, toasted
- Chili powder

DIRECTIONS:

In a pot, place water and rice over medium heat. Add mushrooms, ginger, garlic, Kombu and salt (or Dulse) to the pot. Stir and close the lid. Cook until rice is done, about 30 minutes. Stir a couple of times while it is cooking. Add Bok Choy and simmer for 10 minutes. Ladle into bowls. Serve with toppings.

Butternut Squash Aloo Gobi

Servings: 4 | Amount per Serving: 430g or 14.3 oz.
Preparation Time: 10 minutes | Cooking Time: 20 minutes

INGREDIENTS:

- 4 Tbsp. oil
- 2 medium red onions, sliced
- 4 garlic cloves, crushed
- 2 Tbsp. root ginger, finely grated
- 2 Tbsp. garam masala spice
- 2 tsp. turmeric, ground
- 1 green chili, sliced, de-seeded
- 1 tsp. salt
- 2 cups cherry tomatoes, cut in half
- 2 cups water
- 1 medium butternut squash, peeled, chunks
- 1 small cauliflower florets
- 3/4 cups green beans, cut
- 1 lime zest
- 1 small bunch fresh coriander leaves, chopped

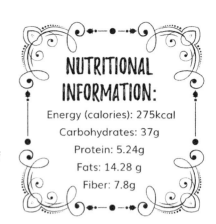

NUTRITIONAL INFORMATION:

Energy (calories): 275kcal
Carbohydrates: 37g
Protein: 5.24g
Fats: 14.28 g
Fiber: 7.8g

DIRECTIONS:

Heat the oil in a large saucepan over medium heat, then add the onions and water sauté with regular stirring for about 10 minutes until lightly browned and they smell savory. Add the spices, garlic, chili and ginger and sauté with constant stirring until aromatic (around 4 minutes). Add the tomatoes, water, butternut squash and salt to the pan. Bring to the boil, then turn down and simmer uncovered for 5 minutes. Add the cauliflower and simmer with the lid on for 10 minutes. Add the green beans and simmer uncovered for 5 minutes, or until the vegetables are tender. Stir in the lime juice and zest, garnish with fresh coriander and serve.

Cauliflower Steaks & Lemon Baked Potato

Servings: 4 | Amount per Serving: 350 g or 11.6 oz.
Preparation Time: 15 minutes | Cooking Time: 90 minutes

INGREDIENTS:

- 1 small head cauliflower, green leaves removed
- 2 Tbsp. extra-virgin olive oil
- 1 tsp. cumin
- 1/2 tsp. coriander
- 1/2 tsp. turmeric
- 1/2 tsp. kosher salt
- 1/4 tsp. black pepper, ground
- 2 small russet potatoes
- 2 Tbsp. almond butter
- 1 small shallot, finely minced
- 2 cloves garlic, minced
- 1 Tbsp. capers
- 1 cup vegetable broth
- Zest and juice of 1 lemon
- 1/4 cup parsley, chopped

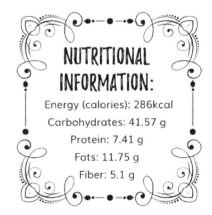

NUTRITIONAL INFORMATION:

Energy (calories): 286kcal
Carbohydrates: 41.57 g
Protein: 7.41 g
Fats: 11.75 g
Fiber: 5.1 g

DIRECTIONS:

Preheat the oven to 425 degrees. Line a baking pan with oiled parchment paper. Cut cauliflower into 1 1/2-inch slices. Place on baking pan. In a small bowl, combine cumin, coriander, turmeric, salt and pepper. Drizzle cauliflower with oil. Rub with spice mixture. Roast for 15 minutes then flip slices and continue cooking for another 15 minutes until golden brown and slightly charred. While roasting the cauliflower, add potatoes to another baking pan and bake for 50 to 60 minutes, until easily pierced with a fork. In a skillet over medium heat, add small amount of water. Add the shallot and garlic and water sauté for 3 minutes. Add the capers, salt, pepper and stock. Bring to simmer and allow liquid to reduce slightly. Turn off heat. Stir in lemon juice, zest, and parsley. Cut slits on top of hot baked potatoes. Pour sauce over steaks and potatoes. Serve immediately.

CASSEROLES

Meatless Loaf

Servings: 4 | Amount per Serving: 230 g or 7.6 oz.
Preparation Time: 15 minutes | Cooking Time: 35 minutes

INGREDIENTS:

- 1 cup Bulgur, cooked
- 1 cup pumpkin flour
- 1 cup of rolled oats
- ½ cup fire-roasted tomatoes, with juice
- 1 small onion, diced
- 1 tsp. minced garlic
- 2 celery stalks, diced
- 2 carrots, diced
- 1/2 green bell pepper, diced
- 1/4 cup walnuts, finely chopped
- 1 ½ Tbsp. of soy sauce
- 1 tsp. Dijon mustard
- ¼ tsp. dried thyme
- ¼ tsp. dried sage
- ¼ tsp. black pepper, ground
- Sea salt, to your taste
- 2 Tbsp. of tomato paste plus enough to top the loaf before baking

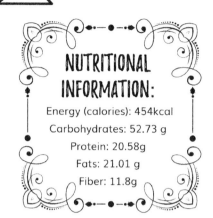

NUTRITIONAL INFORMATION:

Energy (calories): 454kcal

Carbohydrates: 52.73 g

Protein: 20.58g

Fats: 21.01 g

Fiber: 11.8g

DIRECTIONS:

Cook bulgur according to package directions. Cooks on the stove or in a rice cooker in about 15-minutes. Preheat oven to 350 degrees. Line 8×8 baking dish with parchment paper. Dice the veggies--onion, garlic, celery, bell pepper, carrots, & walnuts. Combine all ingredients in a large bowl (including the fully-cooked bulgur). Mix with a spoon, mix thoroughly. Press into prepared dish. Poke holes all over the top, then spread a thin layer of tomato paste over the top with a spatula. Bake for 35 minutes. Serve.

Baked Okra with Veggies

Servings: 4 | Amount per Serving: 480g or 12.3 oz.
Preparation Time: 10 minutes | Cooking Time: 25 minutes

INGREDIENTS:

- 3 lbs. of okra, rinsed and dried
- 6 Tbsp. olive oil
- 3 tsp. fresh thyme
- 1 tsp. garlic powder
- 1 tsp. sea salt
- Ground pepper, to taste
- Pinch of cayenne pepper (optional)
- 2 bell peppers, cut into strips
- 4 cups of broccoli, bite sized

NUTRITIONAL INFORMATION:

Energy (calories): 239kcal

Carbohydrates: 27.1g

Protein: 6.94g

Fats: 14.26g

Fibers: 11.3g

DIRECTIONS:

Preheat oven to 450°F. Trim the okra by cutting away the stem ends and the tips. Then cut the okra in half, lengthwise. Place okra, broccoli and pepper strips in a large bowl. Add oil and spices and stir to coat the okra halves. Place coated veggies on a baking sheet in a single layer. Roast in the oven for 20-25 minutes, shaking or stirring the veggies at least twice during the roasting time. You'll know the okra is ready when it's lightly browned and tender. Serve hot — they tend to lose the crispy texture as they cool. Serve with Asian Salad as a side dish.

Lentil Loaf with Steamed Veggies

Servings: 4 | Amount per Serving: 330g or 10 oz.
Preparation Time: 15 minutes | Cooking Time: 90 minutes

NUTRITIONAL INFORMATION:

Energy (calories): 446kcal
Carbohydrates: 65.44 g
Protein: 20.96g
Fats: 17.32 g
Fibers: 14.1g

INGREDIENTS:

- 1 cup dry lentils
- 2 ½ cups vegetable broth
- 3 Tbsp. flaxseed meal
- 1/3 cup water
- 2 Tbsp. olive oil
- 3 garlic cloves, minced
- 1 small onion, finely diced
- 1 tsp. dried thyme
- ½ tsp. cumin
- ¾ cup oats
- 1 small red bell pepper, finely diced
- 1 carrot, finely diced or grated
- 1 celery stalk, finely diced
- ½ cup oat flour or finely ground oats
- ½ tsp. each garlic powder & onion powder
- ¼ – ½ tsp. ground chipotle pepper, optional
- Cracked pepper & sea salt to taste

DIRECTIONS:

Rinse the lentils, remove odd pieces. In large pot add 2 ½ cups broth with lentils. Bring to a boil, reduce heat, cover and simmer for about 35 – 40 minutes, stirring occasionally. Once done, remove lid and set aside to cool. Lentils will thicken a bit upon standing, about 15 minutes. Preheat oven to 350 degrees. Make flax egg: In small bowl combine flaxseed meal and ⊠ cup water, set aside for at least 10 minutes, preferably in the refrigerator. Water sauté vegetables & spices: In sauté pan heat water over medium heat. Water sauté garlic, onion, bell pepper, carrots and celery for about 5 minutes. Add spices mixing well to incorporate. Set aside to cool. Mash the lentils: Using an immersion blender, food processor, back of a fork or potato masher, blend ¾ of the lentil mixture. Combine sautéed vegetables with the lentils, oats, oat flour and flax-egg, mix well. Taste, adding salt and pepper as needed. Place mixture into a loaf pan lined with parchment paper, leaving it overlapping for easy removal later. Press down firmly filling in along the edges too. Place in center of the oven, and bake in oven for about 45 – 50 minutes. Let cool a bit before slicing. Serve with Avocado Spinach Dip

---

Mary's Italian Eggplant Casserole

Servings: 4

INGREDIENTS:

- 1 large eggplant, chopped
- 1 onion, chopped
- 2 clove garlic, crushed
- 1 green bell pepper, chopped, seeded
- 1 jalapeño pepper, minced (optional)
- 2 oz. olive oil
- 1 can stewed tomato
- 1 can red kidney beans, drained
- 1 Tbsp. Italian spice
- Salt and pepper to taste

DIRECTIONS:

Use oil to coat a Pyrex casserole dish. Add all ingredients and bake at 375 °F for 30 minutes or until eggplant is cooked. Serve with minced scallions as a garnish. Enjoy!

Buffalo Cauliflower Casserole

Servings: 4 | Amount per Serving: 500g or 16.6 oz.
Preparation Time: 10 minutes | Cooking Time: 45 minutes

INGREDIENTS:

- 1 cauliflower head
- 2 individual stalks of kale, roughly chopped
- 1 cup of spinach, roughly chopped

Homemade Spicy Buffalo Cream Sauce:
- ½ cup cashews
- 1 red bell pepper
- 1 Tbsp. apple cider vinegar
- 6 sun-dried tomatoes, pre-soaked

- 2 tsp. garlic powder
- 2 tsp. onion powder
- ½ tsp. cayenne pepper
- ½ cup water
- ¼ tsp. salt

Vegan Garlic 'Cheeze' Sauce:
- ½ cup cashews
- 1 garlic clove
- 1 Tbsp. lemon juice, fresh
- 2 Tbsp. tapioca powder
- 1 tsp. onion powder
- ¼ tsp. salt
- ½ cup water

NUTRITIONAL INFORMATION:
Energy (calories): 318kcal
Carbohydrates: 38.1 g
Protein: 13.18g
Fats: 16.54 g
Fibers: 7.9g

DIRECTIONS:

Cut cauliflower into florets, add to pot of water and bring to a boil for 15 to 20 minutes or until tender. In the meantime, preheat the oven to 350°F.
Make Spicy Buffalo Cream Sauce: Mix all ingredients in a blender until smooth and set aside. Drain cauliflower florets and coat with Spicy Buffalo Cream Sauce. Place coated cauliflower in casserole dish and roast in the oven for 20 minutes.

Make The Vegan Garlic Cheese Sauce: Mix all ingredients in the blender until smooth, set aside. Chop the kale and spinach if not chopped yet. Remove cauliflower from the oven when finished and top with chopped kale and spinach, and pour vegan garlic cheese sauce on top of greens. Place casserole dish back in the oven (on the 2nd rack preferably) and roast at 350°F for another 10 minutes. Remove, let cool, and serve.

Easy Jackfruit Quinoa Bake

Servings: 4 | Amount per Serving: 400 g or 13.3 oz.
Preparation Time: 10 minutes | Cooking Time: 50 minutes

INGREDIENTS:

- 2 cans of jackfruit in water
- 7 oz. of uncooked quinoa
- ½ onion, finely chopped
- 4 Tbsp. soy sauce (unsweetened)
- 3 Tbsp. sweet chili sauce

- 3 Tbsp. tomato paste
- 2 tsp. miso paste
- 3 tsp. BBQ seasoning
- 2 tsp. minced garlic
- 1 quart of boiling water

NUTRITIONAL INFORMATION:
Energy (calories): 414 kcal
Carbohydrates: 88.53 g
Protein: 10 g
Fats: 3.54 g
Fiber: 6.3 g

DIRECTIONS:

Preheat your oven to 390°F. Then drain 2 cans of jackfruit. Chop into bite-size pieces and add them to a baking dish. Wash quinoa. Make sure you wash it well as it's much easier to digest. Add the quinoa to the baking dish, together with the rest of the ingredients including boiling water (it's important that the water is boiling because otherwise it will take longer for the Jackfruit Quinoa Bake to cook thoroughly). Stir well with a wooden spoon and then bake in the oven for 50 min - or until the water has evaporated and just before the edges start to get burnt. Serve with a steamed broccoli on the side. Enjoy!

Chipotle Brown Rice Bake

Servings: 4 | Amount per Serving: 550g or 18.3 oz.
Preparation Time: 15 minutes | Cooking Time: 45 minutes

INGREDIENTS:

- 2 cups short grain brown rice
- 15 oz. black beans, cooked
- 1 cup red onion, diced
- 1 cup corn, frozen
- 1 cup chopped kale or spinach pieces, frozen
- ½ cup black olives, sliced
- 1 chipotle pepper in adobo sauce, diced, seeds removed
- 1 tsp. cumin, ground
- 1 tsp. sea salt, to taste
- ½ tsp. dried oregano
- 3 cups vegetable broth, heated to boiling hot
- 15 oz. tomato sauce
- ½ large avocado, diced
- Lime wedges, optional

NUTRITIONAL INFORMATION:
Energy (calories): 638kcal
Carbohydrates: 121.28 g
Protein: 21.88g
Fats: 9.6 g
Fibers: 19.9g

DIRECTIONS:

Preheat oven to 350°F and line a 9x13-inch baking dish with oiled parchment paper. Next, dump rice, black beans, onion, corn, kale, olives, chipotle pepper, adobo sauce, cumin, salt, and oregano into the baking dish. Stir it together to evenly combine, and then add vegetable broth and tomato sauce, stirring again to evenly combine. Cover dish with aluminum foil and bake for 40 minutes. Then, take dish out, give it a stir, cover with foil again and bake for 20 more minutes. If the rice looks to be cooked through, remove foil from dish and bake for another 10 minutes. Once the baking is done, take it out of the oven and wait 5 minutes before topping with avocado and green onion. Squeeze a lime wedge over the top and enjoy! *If you do not have low or no-sodium vegetable broth/bouillon on hand, just adjust the salt added to 1/4 tsp. or to taste. Serve with cucumber salad
Chef's Note: If you don't have lime or lemon wedges on hand, try stirring 2-3 tsp. (10 ml) white vinegar into the ingredients before baking. The acid really helps balance the flavors.

Coconut and Peanut Aubergine Curry

Servings: 4 | Preparation Time: 10 minutes | Cooking Time: 20-30 minutes

INGREDIENTS:

- 2 aubergines (eggplants), cut into large chunks
- 2 onions, chopped
- 2 garlic cloves, crushed
- Ginger a 2 inch piece, finely grated
- 1 tsp. cumin seeds
- 1 tsp. coriander seeds, crushed
- 1 tsp. turmeric
- ½ tsp. chili powder
- 1 ½ cups half-fat coconut milk
- 1 Tbsp. tamarind paste
- 1 Tbsp. peanut butter

DIRECTIONS:

Heat 1 tsp. oil in a saucepan and add aubergine. Water sauté aubergine until golden brown. Transfer the aubergine to a plate. Heat 2 tsp. water in the same pan and add onion, water sauté until golden brown. Stir in ginger and garlic and cook for one minute. Add all the spices and cook for 2 minutes. Add coconut milk, peanut butter and tamarind to the gravy. Let it simmer until completely mixed. Add aubergine to the pan and cook for 15 minutes. Garnish with coriander and serve warm.

Eggplant Casserole with Beans and Quinoa

Servings: 4 | Amount per Serving: 490 g or 16.3 oz.
Preparation Time: 20 minutes | Cooking Time: 40 minutes

INGREDIENTS:

- 2 large eggplants, whole
- 2 Tbsp. of water, for sauté
- 2 onions finely chopped
- 1 can of cannellini beans, including the water
- 2 garlic cloves, finely chopped
- 1 red/green chili pepper small, finely chopped
- 1 bay leaf
- 1 celery stalk, finely chopped
- 2 large tomatoes, chopped
- 2 Tbsp. tomato paste
- 4 sun-dried tomatoes finely chopped
- 4 Tbsp. white wine
- Sea salt and pepper to taste
- 2 ½ cups of quinoa, cooked

NUTRITIONAL INFORMATION:

Energy (calories): 645 kcal

Carbohydrates: 110.19 g

Protein: 26.01 g

Fats: 13.46 g

Fiber: 27.1 g

DIRECTIONS:

Preheat the oven to 400 F. Place the eggplant on a baking tray and bake for 35 minutes. Remove from the oven, cut off the end and chop the eggplant into chunks (do not remove the skin). Keep the oven on. About 25 minutes into baking the eggplant start preparing the other ingredients. Heat water in a pan over medium high heat for 1 1/2 to 2 minutes or until very warm (hot enough to sizzle). Add diced onions and stir. The bottom of the onions and the pan should begin to brown within about 1 minute. Continue cooking, stirring often, and allow onions to brown, than add a few more spoons of water and cook for another 2-3 minutes stirring often. Add the bay leaf, garlic, chili and celery, stir and cook over a medium heat for 3 minutes, stirring often. Add the wine and continue cooking for 2 more minutes. Add the chopped eggplant, tomato, tomato paste, sun-dried tomatoes, salt, stir, cover and bring to the boil then simmer for 10 minutes. Remove the bay leaf and partly blitz the sauce so that it has a chunky (not completely pureed), consistency (use a stick blender). Combine with the beans with water, stir, and season to taste and transfer into your baking dish and bake for 20 minutes in a preheated oven. Serve with cooked quinoa. Enjoy!

Taro Yellow Coconut Curry

Servings: 4 | Preparation Time: 15 minutes | Cooking Time: 20 minutes

INGREDIENTS:

- 2 ½ cups (500 grams) cubed taro
- Salt
- 4 cups coconut milk
- 4 green chilis pounded lightly
- 8 garlic cloves pounded lightly
- 1 inch ginger pounded lightly
- 2 black cardamoms pounded lightly
- 1 teaspoon turmeric powder

DIRECTIONS:

Remove skin of taro, wash well and cut into small cubes or pieces. Heat water in a pan; add ginger, garlic, black cardamoms, and green chilis and water sauté for half a minute. Next, add turmeric powder and taro and sauté for 2 minutes. Then add the rest of the ingredients and boil over simmering heat until soft and done. Serve hot.

Mimi's Cabbage Casserole

Servings: 4 | Preparation Time: 10 minutes | Cooking Time: 90 minutes

INGREDIENTS:

- 1 head cabbage, chopped
- 1 onion, chopped
- 2 Tbsp. sweet paprika
- 1 tsp. black pepper, ground
- 1 cup water
- 2 Tbsp. olive oil
- 3 bay leaves
- 1 can crushed tomato
- 1 Tbsp. vinegar

DIRECTIONS:

Chop cabbage, place in casserole dish, add spices and massage (squeeze) cabbage to break the cellulose fibers. Add the rest of the ingredients and water. Mix and bake at 375°F for about 90 minutes. Take from the oven and serve.

Mimi's Green Beans Potato Casserole

Servings: 4 | Preparation Time: 10 minutes | Cooking Time: 60 minutes

INGREDIENTS:

- 2 lbs. potatoes, peeled, chopped
- 3 medium onions, chopped
- 2 leeks, chopped
- 2 lbs. green beans
- 1 can stewed tomatoes
- 1 carrot, chopped
- 1 Tbsp. paprika
- 1 tsp. spearmint, dried herb
- 2 Tbsp. olive oil
- 1 oz. parsley, chopped, to garnish
- 1 oz. dill, chopped, to garnish

DIRECTIONS:

Strain tomatoes and mix the tomato juice with vegetable broth, paprika, all the vegetables, except tomatoes, and place in casserole dish. Mix and bake at 375°F for 50-60 minutes until the liquid evaporates. Cover with tomatoes, parsley and dill and bake additional 10 minutes. Serve.

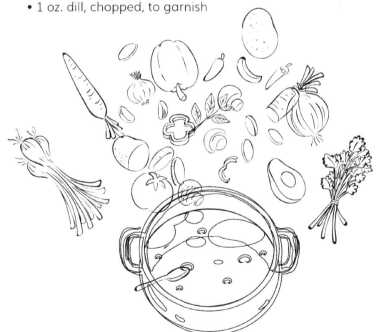

Stuffed Eggplant

Servings: 4 | Preparation Time: 10 minutes | Cooking Time: 90 minutes

INGREDIENTS:

- 2 large eggplants, cut in half lengthwise, flesh scooped out

For the Stuffing:
- 1 medium onion, minced
- 4 mushrooms, minced
- 1 handful walnuts, chopped
- Eggplant flesh, chopped
- 1/3 cup sun dried tomato

- 2 small tomatoes, minced
- 2 handfuls spinach
- 1 Tbsp. Italian spice
- Salt and pepper to taste
- 4 oz. olive oil, divided in half

DIRECTIONS:

Cut eggplant lengthwise, scoop out center meat and place both parts in salt water for 30 minutes. Drain the water, rinse eggplant and rub eggplant with a mix of 2 oz. olive oil and spices. Chop the scooped eggplant and add the rest of the veggies to make a stuffing mix. Add some of the marinade from sun dried tomatoes to mix. Place stuffing mix into each of the 4 halves of eggplant. Place in oiled casserole dish, cover and bake at 400°F for 40-50 minutes. Remove cover the last 10 minutes of cooking time. Serve and enjoy.

Chef's Note: Some eggplants release water while cooking and others do not. Check halfway through baking and if it is dry, add some liquid to keep moist.

Zucchini Boat with Roasted Veggies

Servings: 4 | Amount per Serving: 340g or 11.3 oz.
Preparation Time: 15 minutes | Cooking Time: 40 minutes

INGREDIENTS:

- 4 small to medium zucchini squash
- 6 Tbsp. water
- 2 onions, chopped
- 4 garlic cloves minced
- 2 cups sweet red pepper, diced
- 2 cups diced Cremini mushrooms, diced
- 1 tsp. dried oregano

- 1 tsp. dried basil
- 4 Tbsp. fresh chopped parsley
- 1 tsp. salt
- ¼ tsp. freshly ground black pepper
- 1 cup walnuts
- 1/2 cup of sesame seeds
- 4 Tbsp. of sunflower seeds
- 4 Tbsp. of pumpkin seeds

NUTRITIONAL INFORMATION:

Energy (calories): 619kcal

Carbohydrates: 27.47 g

Protein: 16.4g

Fats: 53.57 g

Fibers: 9.7g

DIRECTIONS:

Preheat oven to 375 degrees. Trim stem end from squash. Cut about 1/3 off the top of each squash horizontally. Then cut a small horizontal sliver from the bottom so that the squash will sit flat and not roll. Dice the tops to ½ inch dice and set aside. Using a small paring knife, cut around inside of squash then using a melon-baller, scoop out inside until the squash resembles a canoe. Try not to cut through to the bottom. In a large skillet or frying pan heat the water over medium heat. Add onion and cook two minutes. Add garlic, red pepper, mushrooms and cut up zucchini tops. Mix to combine and sauté one minute. Remove from heat and mix in oregano, basil, parsley, salt, pepper, seeds. Mix to combine. Divide the filling between each zucchini boat and press into squash filling and pressing as you fill to hold shape. Bake for 35 – 40 minutes uncovered. Try not to overcook, otherwise the zucchini will start to sag and the filling will not stay in.

Build Your Own Delicious Clay Pot Meal

WHAT IS A CLAY POT MEAL?

Clay pots have been used around the world by nearly every culture for thousands of years. Today, they can be used to provide a tasty, "all-in-one", layered meal that that can be personalized to your liking. For example, you could make 4 different clay pot cuisines at once and share with you guests. You could make one Asian cuisine, one Moroccan cuisine, one Russian cuisine and one American cuisine and share it like an international buffet!

BEST TIPS FOR HANDLING YOUR CLAY POT.

• Never put your clay pot in a preheated oven because it will crack from the shock of the heat. It must be heated slowly. Place in a cold oven.
• When you take it from the oven, place the clay pot on a wood surface or potholder. Do not place it on a hard cool surface as it will crack the pot.
• Clay pots should not be used on the stove top.
• When filling the pot with your ingredients, leave room at the top so it does not overflow when cooking.
• When you take it from the oven, the clay pot will retain heat for up to 30 minutes. Please let it cool for a while before eating.

HOW TO CLEAN YOUR CLAY POT

The best way to clean your clay pot is using a soft bristle brush using warm water and a little baking soda. Since the clay pot is porous, using soap may allow it to absorb the soap and give your future meals a soapy taste.

HOW TO BUILD YOUR CLAY POT

Here are some inspirational ideas and a step-by-step guide to get you started. With clay pot cooking, you will find that when you let your creativity flow, you will experience an endless array of dazzling tastes.

It is best to build your clay pot meal in layers. You can use any veggie ingredients you like. Here is how to do it:

STEP 1: Rinse your clay pot to be sure it is clean.
STEP 2: First, choose your oil, (olive, grapeseed, sunflower, etc.) and add a little oil to the pot just to have a thin coating on the bottom.
STEP 3: Add chopped onions, garlic, ginger, etc.
STEP 4: Choose your hard root veggies like chopped potato, sweet potato, taro, yucca, carrots, turnips, celery, parsnips, etc.
STEP 5: Choose your legumes: (should be pre-cooked) beans, lentils edamame, etc.
STEP 6: Choose your soft veggies: peppers, eggplant, broccoli, cauliflower, cabbage, corn, mushrooms, zucchini, greens, olives, etc.
STEP 7: Choose your sauce: BBQ, veggie broth, soy sauce, curry sauce, Dijon mustard, etc.
STEP 8: Add your favorite spices.

HOW TO COOK YOUR CLAY POT MEAL

Place in a cold oven and heat to 400°F for 45-50 minutes for a small (individual meal) clay pot or 60-75 minutes for larger pots.

Note: Please remember that you must NOT place in preheated oven because the sudden temperature change will crack your clay pot and you will have a terrible mess to clean up.

You can eat your clay pot meal directly from the pot or scoop it onto a plate. Just remember that if you eat it from the pot, it will stay very hot for some time so be careful you do not burn your tongue eating it. Eating from the pot has a certain charm and reminds us of our distant ancestors, who did the same.

SAMPLE CLAY POT RECIPES

Potato Mushroom Clay Pot

Servings: 4 | Amount per Serving: 14 oz.
Preparation Time: 10 minutes | Cooking Time: 45 minutes

INGREDIENTS:

- 1 Tbsp. oil
- 2 cloves garlic, crushed
- ½ onion, chopped
- 1 large potato, peeled, diced
- 4 mushrooms, sliced
- 1 green bell pepper, sliced
- 4 oz. vegetable broth
- ½ tsp. Italian spice
- Salt and pepper to taste

NUTRITIONAL INFORMATION:

Energy (calories): 367kcal
Carbohydrates: 37.33 g
Protein: 9.68 g
Fat: 21.76 g
Fiber 12.7g

DIRECTIONS:

Add oil to the pot, followed by layers of onions, garlic, potato, mushrooms, bell peppers and vegetable broth. Cover with lid and place in cold oven. Heat oven to 400°F and cook for about 45 minutes until potatoes are done. Remove from oven and place on potholder for 15 minutes to cool. Season with salt and pepper to taste. Serve and enjoy.

Veggie Medley Clay Pot

Servings: 4 | Amount per Serving: 14 oz.
Preparation Time: 10 minutes | Cooking Time: 45 minutes

INGREDIENTS:

- 1 Tbsp. oil
- 2 cloves garlic, crushed
- ½ onion, chopped
- 4 florets cauliflower
- ¼ cup corn, frozen
- ¼ cup red bell pepper, sliced
- ¼ cup edamame
- ¼ cup garbanzo beans, cooked
- ¼ cup green beans, cut
- ½ stalk celery, sliced
- 3 oz. vegetable broth
- 1 Tbsp. tomato paste
- 1 tsp. Sazon spice
- Salt and pepper to taste

DIRECTIONS:

Add oil to the pot, followed by layers of onions, garlic, onion, cauliflower, corn, peppers, green beans, edamame, celery, garbanzo beans, tomato paste, Sazon and vegetable broth. Mix, Cover with lid and place in cold oven. Heat oven to 400°F and cook for about 45 minutes until done. Remove from oven and place on potholder for 15 minutes to cool. Season with salt and pepper to taste. Serve and enjoy.

Chickpea Potato Curry Clay Pot

Servings: 1 | Preparation Time: 5 minutes | Cooking Time: 15 minutes

INGREDIENTS:

- 1/2 cup chickpeas, cooked
- 1/2 cup potatoes, cubed
- Salt to taste
- Pepper to taste
- 1/3 tsp. garlic powder
- 1/3 tsp. ginger powder
- 1 tsp. lemon juice
- ¼ tsp. chili flakes
- 2 Tbsp. vegetable stock
- 1 tsp. olive oil

DIRECTIONS:

Combine all ingredients in a clay pot. Put on the lid. Place in cold oven and bake at 400 °F in oven for 40 minutes until potatoes are done. Do not place clay pot meals in a pre-heated oven as the pot will break and leave you with a mess to clean. Take out of oven and place on a potholder to cool for 15 minutes. Serve.

Sample Meal Plans With Shopping Lists

SHOPPING LIST FOR DANIEL FAST WEEK 1

FRUITS
Apple, 11 pcs.
Avocado, 7 pcs.
Banana, 5 medium +2 large
Blueberry 4.5 cups
Grapes, 1 cup
Kiwifruit, 4 pcs.
Lemon, 3 pcs.
Lime, 5 pcs.
Mango, 1 pcs.
Orange, 6 large
Pineapple 2 cups
Raspberries, 1 cup
Strawberries, 6 cups

SPICES & HERBS
BBQ seasoning
Black pepper
White Pepper
Chili powder
Cinnamon
Cumin, ground, 4 Tbsp.
Garlic powder
Ginger
Italian Seasoning
Oregano
Coriander
Fennel Seeds
Turmeric, dried
Dill

STAPLES
Dijon mustard, 2 tsp.
Salt, Sea
Vanilla extract, 2.5 tsp.
Seeds oil, 5 Tbsp.
Olive Oil
Avocado oil
Sushi vinegar
Japanese soy sauce 4 Tbsp.
Baking soda
Roasted tahini 2-3 Tbsp.
Apple cider vinegar

FROZEN FOODS
Mixed berries, 4 cups
Blueberry, 3 cups
Cantaloupe, 2 cups (360g)
Peas, 4 lbs.
Mango-Peach, 2 cups

DRIED FRUIT, NUTS, & SEEDS
Almonds 2 cups +4 Tbsp.
Chia seeds, 9 oz.
Cranberries, dried, 2 Tbsp.
Dates, dried, 5 oz. + 8 pcs
Flaxseeds, 22 Tbsp.
Hazelnuts, 1 cup
Pecans, ° cup
Pumpkin seeds, 2 Tbsp.
Raisins 3 Tbsp. (50g)
Sesame seeds, 8Tbsp.
Sunflower seeds, 2 Tbsp.
Walnuts, 3.5 cups (1 lbs.)
Pumpkin flour, 1 cup

PACKAGED ITEMS
Almond butter smooth, 2 Tbsp.
Peanut butter, 1 oz.
Tomato paste, 4 Tbsp.
Tomato juice, 27 fl oz.
Tomato, roasted, canned, 29 oz.
Vegetable broth, 6 qt
Sunflower Butter, ° cup
Sauerkraut, optional topping
Black beans, 1 lbs.
Almond milk, 3.5 cups
Kalamata olives, 8 oz.

GRAINS & PRODUCTS
Oats, rolled, 4 cups, (1.2 lbs.)
Quinoa, 40 oz. (2.6 lbs.)
Rice, brown, 12 oz.
Millet 5 oz.
Potato buns, 4 pcs.
Bulgur, 1 cup

VEGETABLES
Alfalfa sprouts, 1 Tbsp.
zucchinis
Arugula, 4 cups (80g)
Bean sprouts (1.6 lbs.)
Beans, Black, 11 oz.
Beans, Green, 2 lbs.
Beans, white, 11 oz.
Bell pepper, 8 medium (1.7 lbs.)
Broccoli, 2 lbs.
Butternut squash 1.6 oz.(48g)
Cabbage, head, 2 small
Carrots, 3.5 lbs.
Celery stalk, 9 large (1.5 lbs.)
Chickpeas, 4 lbs.
Cilantro, 6 cups (90g)
Coleslaw mix, 8 oz.
Cucumber 6 medium (2.3 lbs.)
Eggplant, 1-2 (2 lbs.)
Garlic, 23 cloves
Ginger, 1î inch pcs,
Lentils, green 7 oz. (210g)
Lentils, red, 1 cup
Lettuce 3 heads, small (1.2 lbs.)
Mixed Greens, 2 cups (40g)
MungBeans, 1 cup
Mushrooms shiitake, 1.8 oz.
Mushrooms, 21 oz.(630g)
Onion, 10 medium
Parsley or Basil, fresh, 2 cups
Pepper, chilli, 3 pcs.
Portobello mushroom, 2 large (170g)
Potatoes, sweet, 1
Radishes, 18 pcs.
Scallions or shallots, or spring16pcs.
Spinach, 12 cups (360g)
Tomatoes, 4 lbs.
Watercress, 4 cups (140g)
Zucchini 5 pcs. or 2.3 lbs.

SAMPLE MEAL PLAN WEEK 1

	DAY 1	DAY 2	DAY 3	DAY 4	DAY 5	DAY 6	DAY 7
I MEAL	**1 SERVING OF** Ireland Apple Berry Smoothie	**1 SERVING OF** Granola with Fruit and Almond Milk	**1 SERVING OF** Love Berry Kiwi Smoothie	**1 SERVING OF** Berry Chia Breakfast Bowl	**1 SERVING OF** Banana Porridge	**1 SERVING OF** Ola Mango Peach Smoothie	**1 SERVING OF** Sweet Potato Toast with Baba Ganesh
DESSERTS & SNACKS	**1 ORANGE**	**1 SERVING OF** Apple Tart with Nuts	**1 CUP OF BLUE BERRIES**	**1 APPLE**	**2 CUPS OF PINEAPPLE**	**1 LARGE BANANA**	**1 ORANGE**
II MEAL	**1 SERVING OF** Quinoa veggie Bowl and **1 SERVING OF** Steamed Broccoli	**1 SERVING OF** Meat Free Meatballs and **1 SERVING OF** Spinach Mashed Potatoes Salad	**1 SERVING OF** Brown Rice & beans with grilled Portobello mushrooms & **1 SERVING OF** Sesame Green Beans	**1 SERVING OF** Raw Pad Thai Bowl	**1 SERVING OF** Peas Potato Stew and **1 SERVING OF** Lettuce & Radish salad	**1 SERVING OF** Hawaiian Poke Garden Bowl	**1 SERVING OF** BBQ Jackfruit Sandwiches
III MEAL	**1 SERVING OF** Moroccan Vegetable Stew with ½ **SERVING OF** Nut Bread	**1 SERVING OF** Paradise Garden Asian Bowl	**1 SERVING OF** Spiced carrot & lentil soup & **1 SERVING OF** Vegan style Greek Salad	**1 SERVING OF** Vegan Chickpeas burger & **1 SERVING** of Watercress and lettuce salad with seeds	**1 SERVING OF** Minestrone soup & **1 SERVING** of Mediterranean Zucchini Noodles Pasta	**1 SERVING OF** Lazy Cabbage Rolls with Mung Beans **1/2 SERVING** or 1 slice of Quinoa & Chia Bread	**1 SERVING OF** Vegan Meat Loaf with **1 SERVING** of Cabbage Salad
	WHOLE DAY KCAL	**WHOLE DAY KCAL**	**WHOLE DAY KCAL**	**WHOLE DAY KCAL**	**WHOLE DAY KCAL**	**WHOLE DAY KCAL**	**WHOLE DAY KCAL**
	1527	1776	1564	1507	1576	1667	1673

DAILY AVERAGE - 1613 KCAL

SHOPPING LIST FOR DANIEL FAST WEEK II

FRUITS
Apple, 2 pcs.
Avocado, 3 pcs.
Banana, 15 medium
Blueberry 1 cup
Lemon, 4 pcs.
Lime, 1 pcs.
Orange, 1 large
Papaya, 1 pcs
Pear, 1 medium
Pomegranate arils, 2 Tbsp
Strawberries, 3 cup

SPICES & HERBS
Bay leaves, 3 pcs.
BBQ seasoning
Black pepper
Chili powder
Cinnamon
Coriander
Cumin, ground, 2Tbsp
Garam masala, ° tsp.
Garlic powder
Mexican Seasoning
Onion powder
Tapioca powder

STAPLES
Apple cider vinegar
Avocado oil
Chilli sauce, 3 Tbsp
Coconut Oil, 1 Tbsp
Dijon mustard, 1 tsp.
Dijon mustard, 2 tsp.
Olive Oil
Salt, Sea
Seeds oil, 4 Tbsp.
Soy Sauce 4 Tbsp
Vanilla extract, 10 tsp.
White wine, 4 Tbsp.

FROZEN FOODS
Blueberry, 4 cups
Peas, 1cup
Mango-Peach, 2 cups
Corn, 2.7 lbss.

DRIED FRUIT, NUTS, & SEEDS
Cashews 1 cup (150g)
Chia seeds, 8 oz.
Dates, dried, 4 pcs
Figs, dried, 6 oz.
Flax meal, 2.5 oz.
Flaxseeds, 10 Tbsp
Pecans, 1.7 oz.
Pine Nuts, 6 Tbsp
Poppy Seeds, 2 oz.
Prunes, Dried, 6 pcs.
Pumpkin seeds, 6 oz.
Sesame seeds, 1.7 oz.
Sunflower seeds, 6 Tbsp.
Tahini 2 oz.
Walnuts, 7.7 oz.

PACKAGED ITEMS
Almond milk, 10 cups
Jackfruit, 25 oz.
Miso paste 2 tsp.
Vegan mayo, 1 cup
Granola, ° cup
Sun-dried tomatoes, 25 pcs.
Tomatoes, canned, 14 oz.
Tomato paste, 7 tbsp
Tomato, roasted, canned, 35 oz.

GRAINS & PRODUCTS
Barley pearl, 10 oz.
Chickpeas 15 oz.
Oats, rolled, 8.5 cups, (30 oz.)
Quinoa, 2.3 lbss

VEGETABLES
Arugula, 14 cups (210g)
Beans, Black, 17 oz.
Beans, Green, 3.6 lbss.
Beans, white, 56 oz.
Bell pepper, 19 medium
Cabbage, 5 cups (350g)+2 cups red
Carrots, 1 cup
Cauliflower, Head 1 (600g)
Celery stalk, 6 small +2 large (140g)
Chives, fresh1 Tbsp.
Cucumber 3 medium
Edamame, 1 cup
Eggplants, 1.5 large whole
Garlic, 18 cloves
Kale 2 stalks (35g),
Leek, 1 pcs (120g)
Lentils, brown, ° cup
Lentils, red, 2 cups
Lentils, sprouted 4 oz.
Lettuce, 16 leaves
Mint, fresh, 2 Tbsp.s
Basil, fresh, 2 Tbsp.2
Mixed greens 8 cups (300g)
Mushrooms, 22 oz.
Onion, 10 medium
Parsley or Basil, fresh, 10 Tbsp
Pepper, chilli, 5 pcs.
Potato, yukon 2 small (400g)+6 red
Potatoes, sweet, 8
Scallions or shallots, or spring 20pcs.
Spinach, 2.1 lbss.
Tomatoes, 6 large

SAMPLE MEAL PLAN WEEK II

	DAY 1	DAY 2	DAY 3	DAY 4	DAY 5	DAY 6	DAY 7
I MEAL	**1 SERVING OF** Cinnamon Old Fashion Oatmeal	**1 SERVING OF** Viva Red Smoothie	**1 SERVING OF** Easy Gluten Free Oat Pancakes with spread of dried figs & walnuts	**1 SERVING OF** Chia ñ Papaya & dried prunes pudding	**1 SERVING OF** Sweet Potato Waffles with Banana-Straw berries Spread	**1 SERVING OF** Smoothie Bowl with Berries & Granola	**1 SERVING OF** Energy Green Bliss Smoothie
DESSERTS & SNACKS	**1 MEDIUM APPLE**	**1 PEAR**	**1 MANDARIN ORANGE**	**1 CUP OF BLUE BERRIES**	**1 LARGE BANANA**	**1 APPLE**	**1 ORANGE**
II MEAL	**1 SERVING OF** Quinoa Nut Pilaf Salad	**1 SERVING OF** Indiana Succotash	**1 SERVING OF** Black Bean Hummus Burrito	**1 SERVING OF** Lettuce Wrap with quinoa & Chipotle Sauce	**1 SERVING OF** Sweet Potato Bowl and **1 SERVING** of Fennel Orange Salad	**1 SERVING OF** Green Bean Salad with Vegan Mayo & **1 SERVING OF** Baked Potato	**1 SERVING OF** Lentil Taco Wrap with Avocado Pico de Gallo
III MEAL	**1 SERVING OF** Spinach Potato Soup **1 SERVING OF** Buffalo Cauliflower Casserole & **½ A SERVING** of Nut Bread	**1 SERVING** of Chili Beans Stew, **1 SERVING** of Cabbage Salad and **½ A SERVING** of Nut	**1 SERVING OF** Easy jackfruit and quinoa bake	**1 SERVING OF** Red Lentil Tomato Kale Soup and **1 SERVING OF** Arugula Salad with Seeds	**1 SERVING OF** Jackfruit Lentil Wraps	**1 SERVING OF** Stuffed bell Peppers with Mushrooms & **1 SERVING** of Green Salad with Pomegranate	**1 SERVING OF** Eggplant Casserole with Beans & Quinoa **1 SERVING OF** Chief Salad with greens
	WHOLE DAY KCAL	**WHOLE DAY KCAL**	**WHOLE DAY KCAL**	**WHOLE DAY KCAL**	**WHOLE DAY KCAL**	**WHOLE DAY KCAL**	**WHOLE DAY KCAL**
	1661	1577	1695	1591	1575	1611	1536

DAILY AVERAGE - 1606 KCAL

SHOPPING LIST FOR DANIEL FAST WEEK III

FRUITS
Apple, 1 pcs.
Avocado, 10 pcs.
Banana, 15 medium
Blueberry 2 cups
Figs, 4 pcs
Lemon, 8 pcs.
Lime, 1 pcs.
Mango, 1 pcs
Pear, 1 medium
Pineapple, 3 cups
Pomegranate arils, 4 Tbsp.
Red grapefruit, 1 large pcs.
Strawberries, 2 cups+28pcs
Tangerine, 5 pcs

SPICES & HERBS
Black pepper
Chili powder
Cinnamon
Nutmeg,
Coriander
Cumin, ground, ° tsp.
Garlic powder
Italian Seasoning
Onion powder
Oregano, dried
Dill
Thyme
Garlic powder
Curry powder

STAPLES
Apple cider vinegar
Dijon mustard, ° cup
Olive Oil
Salt, Sea
Seeds oil, 4 Tbsp.
Vanilla extract, 1 tsp.
White vinegar ° cup
Balsamic vinegar, 2 Tbsp.
red wine vinegar, ° cup
Baking soda

FROZEN FOODS
Mixed berries, 4 cups
Blueberry, 3 cups
Cantaloupe, 2 cups (360g)
Peas, 4 lbs.
Mango-Peach, 2 cups

DRIED FRUIT, NUTS, & SEEDS
Almonds 2 cups +4 Tbsp.
Chia seeds, 9 oz.
Cranberries, dried, 2 Tbsp.
Dates, dried, 5 oz. + 8 pcs
Flaxseeds, 22 Tbsp.
Hazelnuts, 1 cup
Pecans, ° cup
Pumpkin seeds, 2 Tbsp.
Raisins 3 Tbsp. (50g)
Sesame seeds, 8Tbsp.
Sunflower seeds, 2 Tbsp.
Walnuts, 3.5 cups (1 lbs.)
Pumpkin flour, 1 cup

PACKAGED ITEMS
Almond Butter, 5 Tbsp.
Almond milk, 10 cups
Capers, 1 Tbsp.
Chipotle pepper in adobo sauce, 1
Olives, black 2 oz.
Peanut butter, 6 Tbsp.
Tamari (soy) sauce, 2 ° Tbsp.s
applesauce, 1 Tbsp.
Tomato, roasted, canned, 28 oz.
Tomatoes, canned, 31 oz.

GRAINS & PRODUCTS
Barley 15 oz.
Brown rice, 2 cups (390g)
Chickpeas 69 oz.
Israeli couscous, 4 oz.
Oats, rolled, 4 cups,
Quinoa, 22.5 oz.

VEGETABLES
Alfalfa sprouts 2 cups (16g)
Arugula, 3 cups
Beans Black, 40 oz.
Beans, white, 9 oz.
Beets, 7 small pcs.
Bell pepper, 7 medium
bok choi, 3.5 oz. 1 avocado, sliced
Broccoli2 cup
Brussels sprouts, 36 oz.
Butternut squash, 1 lbs. skin off,
Cabbage, 4 cups
Carrots, 12 pcs. medium
Cauliflower, Head 1 (600g)
Celery stalk, 6 small
Cilantro, fresh, 2 cups
Collard greens leaves 4 large
Coriander, fresh, 1 Tbsp.
Cucumber, 6 medium
Ear corn husks, 1 pcs
Edamame beans, 3.5 oz.
Eggplants, 3 small
Garlic, 38 cloves
Kale or Collard Greens, 4 cups (350g)
Lentils, brown or green, 2 cups
Mixed salad greens, 6 cups
Mushrooms, 11 oz.
Onion, 6 medium+3 red,
Parsley or Basil, fresh, 7 cups
Pepper, chilli, 2 pcs.
Portobello mushrooms, 4 pcs. ~11 oz.
Potato, 4 pcs. medium
Potatoes, sweet, 2 pcs. large
Pumpkin 16 oz.
Radishes, 10-14 pcs. medium
Rosemary, fresh, 1 tsp.
Scallions, shallots, or spring 11 pcs
Spinach, 27 cups
Tomatoes, 6 large + 30 pcs. cherry

SAMPLE MEAL PLAN WEEK III

	DAY 1	DAY 2	DAY 3	DAY 4	DAY 5	DAY 6	DAY 7
I MEAL	½ SERVING OF Homemade Hummus with Avocado and 1 slice of Nut Bread Toast	1 SERVING OF Glowing Pink Smoothie	1 SERVING OF Barley pudding w/ fruits and nuts	1 SERVING OF Collard Greens Banana wrap	1 SERVING OF OmbrÈ Pineapple Mango Smoothie	1 SERVING OF Delicious Strawberry Oatmeal Smoothie	1 SERVING OF Granola with Fruits
DESSERTS & SNACKS	1 CUP OF PINE APPLE	1 SERVING OF Apple Cake with dried prunes	1 CUP OF BLUE BERRIES	1 MEDIUM PEAR	1 LARGE BANANA	1 APPLE	1 LARGE BANANA
II MEAL	1 SERVING OF Portobello Chickpea Salad	1 SERVING OF Indian Lentil & Collard Soup & **1 SERVING OF** 7 Spice Mediterranean Tabbouleh Salad	1 SERVING OF Roasted Red Pepper Tapenade Sandwich with Alfalfa Sprouts	1 SERVING OF Lemon-Parsley Bean Salad	1 SERVING OF Spicy Quinoa Veggie Bowl	1 SERVING OF Cauliflower Steaks and Lemon Baked Potato	1 SERVING of Roasted Brussels sprouts with Cranberries **1 SERVING** of Mushroom Barley Soup
III MEAL	1 SERVING OF Italian Bean & Kale Soup & **1 SERVING** of Roasted Beet & Spinach Salad	1 SERVING OF Roasted Vegetable Salad with Lime Green Sauce	1 SERVING OF Chipotle Brown Rice Bake and **1 SERVING OF** cucumber salad	1 SERVING OF Lentil Loaf & Steamed Veggies and **1 SERVING OF** Spinach Avocado dip	1 SERVING OF Pumpkin soup and **1 SERVING OF** Eggplant Salad with Roasted Tomatoes	1 SERVING OF Tomato Barley Vegetable Soup with **1 SERVING OF** Mexican Salad	1 SERVING OF Baked Falafel Burgers w/ Many Colors Joseph Salad
	WHOLE DAY KCAL	**WHOLE DAY KCAL**	**WHOLE DAY KCAL**	**WHOLE DAY KCAL**	**WHOLE DAY KCAL**	**WHOLE DAY KCAL**	**WHOLE DAY KCAL**
	1671	1679	1603	1600	1570	1493	1619

DAILY AVERAGE - 1596 KCAL

SHOPPING LIST FOR DANIEL FAST WEEK IV

FRUITS
Apple, 9 pcs.
Avocado, 1 pcs.
Banana, 7 medium
Blueberry 4 cups
Honeydew, 2 cups
Lemon, 5 pcs.
Lime, 3 pcs.
Orange, 2 medium
Pear, 2 medium
Pineapple, 3 cups
Tangerine, 1 pcs

SPICES & HERBS
Basil, dried
Black pepper
Chili powder or flax
Chives
Cinnamon
Cumin, ground,
Curry powder
Dill
Garlic powder
Nutmeg,
Onion powder
Oregano, dried
Shawarma Spice Blend
Pumpkin pie spice
Thyme
Garam masala spice
Turmeric

STAPLES
Baking soda
Balsamic vinegar
Olive Oil
Red wine vinegar, 1 tsp.
Salt, Sea
Seeds oil, 1 Tbsp.
White vinegar 2 tsp.

FROZEN FOODS
Mixed Berries, 1 cups
Corn, 0.5 cup (70g)

DRIED FRUIT, NUTS, & SEEDS
Almond flour, 1 cup
Almonds, 2.8 cups
Chia seeds, 8 oz.
Flax meal, 3.2 oz.
Flaxseeds, 9.5 oz.
Pecans, 2 oz.
Pine Nuts, 2.5 oz.
Prunes, Dried, 4 pcs.
Pumpkin seeds, 8 oz.
Raisins, 2 Tbsp.
Sesame seeds, 6 oz.
Sunflower seeds, 7 oz.
Walnuts, 18 oz.
Dried cranberries 1 oz.
Hazelnuts, ° cup

PACKAGED ITEMS
Almond Butter, 2 Tbsp.
Almond milk, 16 cups
Mild green chilis 1 of 4-oz. can
sheet of nori paper, 2 pcs
sauerkraut, 1 oz.
Olives, Kalamata 2 cups +1
Castelvetrano olives
Salsa Sauce, ° cup
Sun-Dried/Dehydrated
Tomatoes, 4 pcs.
Tamari (soy) sauce, 2 ° Tbsp.s
Tomato purÈe 1cup
Vegetable broth, 6 cups

GRAINS & PRODUCTS
Brown rice, 4.5 cups
Chickpeas 70 oz.
Oats, rolled, 11 cups,
Quinoa, 13.5 oz.

VEGETABLES
Alfalfa sprouts ° cups (16g)
Arugula, 6 cups
Beans Black, 46 oz.
Beets, 3 small pcs.
Bell pepper, 12 medium
Bell, peppers, roasted, 6 pcs
Broccoli, 4 cups
Cabbage, 1.5 cups
Carrots, 16 pcs. medium
Cauliflower, 4, Heads
Celery stalk, 6 small
Cilantro, fresh, 8 stalks
+ 2 cups
Collard greens leaves 4 large
Coriander, fresh 1 small bunch
Cucumber, 6 medium
Garlic, 28 cloves
Ginger, 3 inch pcs
Green beans, 1 cup
Kale or Collard Greens,12 oz.
Leek, 1 pcs
Lentil sprouts, 1 cup
Lentils, brown, green, or red
2.5 cups
Lettuce, 34 oz. + 8 large
leaves
Mushrooms, 10 oz.
Okra, 3 lbs
Onion, 6 medium+ 6 red,
small
Parsley or Basil, fresh, 5 cups
Pepper, chilli, 1 pcs.
Potato, 2 pcs. medium
Pumpkin 2.8 lbs.
Scallions, shallots,
or spring 13 pcs
Spinach, 2 cups
Tomatoes, 10 large +
6 cups cherry
Zucchini squash, 9 medium

SAMPLE MEAL PLAN WEEK IV

	DAY 1	DAY 2	DAY 3	DAY 4	DAY 5	DAY 6	DAY 7
I MEAL	**1 SERVING OF** Deep Green Colada Smoothie	**1 SERVING OF** Green Honeydew smoothie	**1 SERVING OF** Rosemary Walnut Pate	**1 SERVING OF** Rice Pudding w/ seeds, nuts, fruits	**1 SERVING OF** Blueberry Chia Seed Pudding	**1 SERVING OF** Creamy Pumpkin Oats with Blueberries and Toasted Almonds	**1 SERVING OF** Breakfast Baked Apples
DESSERTS & SNACKS	**1 ORANGE**	**2 CUPS OF PINEAPPLE**	**1 PEAR**	**1 MEDIUM APPLE**	**1 TANGERINE**	**1 ORANGE**	**1 LARGE BANANA**
II MEAL	**1 SERVING OF** Opa Greek Paradise Garden Bowl	**1 SERVING OF** Spinach Salad with Citrus and Roasted Beets	**1 SERVING OF** Lentil Kale Salad	**1 SERVING OF** Roasted Chickpea Lettuce Wrap	**1 SERVING OF** Stuffed Bell Peppers with zucchini, mushrooms and rice	**1 SERVING OF** Cranberry Cilantro Quinoa Salad	**1 SERVING OF** Cabbage Detox Soup w/ Salad
III MEAL	**1 SERVING** of Zucchini Boat w/ Roasted Veggies & 1 serving of Green Salad ° serving of Pumpkin Oat Banana Bread	**1 SERVING OF** Potato Corn Chowder with Spicy Black Bean Burger and Mixed Green Salad	**1 SERVING OF** Butternut Squash Aloo Gobi and **1 SLICE OF** Seed Bread	**1 SERVING OF** Baked Okra with Veggies and **1 SERVING** of Asian Salad Recipe with Sesame Ginger Dressing	**1 SERVING** 1 serving of Mexican Green Chili Veggie Burgers,1 slice of Red Lentil Flatbread & 1 serving of Avocado Salad	**1 SERVING** of Cauliflower Leek Soup with **1 SERVING** of Bean Burger Patties and Cucumber Dill Salad	**1 SERVING OF** 1 serving of Buffalo Cauliflower Casserole and **1 SLICE** of Golden Seed Bread
	WHOLE DAY KCAL	**WHOLE DAY KCAL**	**WHOLE DAY KCAL**	**WHOLE DAY KCAL**	**WHOLE DAY KCAL**	**WHOLE DAY KCAL**	**WHOLE DAY KCAL**
	1594	1661	1677	1504	1657	1681	1689

DAILY AVERAGE - 1637 KCAL

MY RECIPES

MY RECIPES

MY RECIPES

MY RECIPES

MY RECIPES

MY RECIPES

MY RECIPES

MY RECIPES

MY RECIPES

MY RECIPES

Printed in Great Britain
by Amazon

37527681R00066